FOUND BY GOD

Christine Murray.
16. North Tolsta.

3rd August 1987.

FOUND BY GOD

Vijay Menon with Derrick Knowlton

Marshalls

Marshalls Paperbacks
Marshall Morgan & Scott
1 Bath Street, London EC1V 9LB

First published by Marshall Morgan & Scott 1982

ISBN: 0 551 00983 7

Photoset in England by
Rowland Phototypesetting Ltd
Printed in England by
Richard Clay (The Chaucer Press) Ltd

Contents

To all my prayer partners

1: Flashpoint

It was a spring day in 1965. Out in the English countryside primroses were blooming along the lanes, lambs were leaping with joy in the fields and the little hedge sparrows were already brooding their young in the thick thorn hedgerows. Everywhere there was renewal and resurgence of new life. Well, not quite everywhere. To my eyes, at least, spring was not very much in evidence in the streets of the City of London.

It was the lunch hour and I, a Hindu, a Lloyd's Surveyor by profession and an ex-marine engineer, was walking from the Bank of England to Liverpool Street. I came to Bishopsgate and noticed with distaste the dull, discoloured blocks of Portland stone in the buildings along this street. They seemed to convey the very atmosphere of the bleak and desolate landscape of the Dorset promontory from which they had been hewn. Stern, hard, unyielding, they were ideal for repelling the onslaught of the waves in their natural habitat and equally as building stones they were perfect for resisting the chemical attacks of the polluted urban air. But they spoke so little of joy. It was all very different from the colourful architecture of my native Kerala.

In my imagination, these stones resembled the long faces of the many Englishmen hurrying past me who appeared to be going nowhere quickly. But who was I to entertain critical thoughts? All my life I had been searching for spiritual reality and in the main, it had eluded me. Hindus take to religion as ducks to water and I was very proud of Hinduism which I was convinced was superior to Christianity. Yet I cannot truthfully say that I had found spiritual happiness. I felt that there was more – so very much more – to be achieved.

Suddenly there was a commotion a little further along the street. On the opposite side there was a narrow archway and through this were pouring hundreds of well-dressed Englishmen, many of them wearing the ritual garb of the City business man, bowler hat, pin-striped suit and the inevitable umbrella. What, I wondered, was going on? Perhaps it was a large fire, or maybe a serious accident?

Consumed with curiosity, I crossed the street and soon found myself borne along on the crest of a human wave which carried me under the arch. We were then in a small courtyard. Immediately ahead was what seemed to be a hall of some kind. The front was battlemented and surmounted by a clock tower and weather-vane. The stones of the front wall were blackened by London's grime. A strange sort of building, perhaps one of the City's ancient livery halls, I thought. The flow was passing through its open doors. This must be a lecture, I decided, and an especially interesting one at that, to attract so many people.

I was handed a pink sheet at the door and on going down the steps I saw a big table on the left-hand side loaded with apples, bananas and sandwiches. No one had asked me for a ticket so evidently there was going to be a free meal into the bargain. I rubbed my hands in gleeful anticipation. The building was rapidly filling up but I was ushered to the middle where there were a couple of seats still vacant.

I sat down and began looking around. In the centre was a line of fluted pillars. All the windows were of stained glass. Ahead were a pulpit, a table and a screen behind which were some tombs. The unpleasant truth dawned on me – I was in a Christian church! My first reaction, I can tell you, was to get out at once. You would not have seen me dead in a church. But it had been difficult enough to get in, and now that I was jammed in, it was virtually impossible to get out! I looked around at the sea of faces. As I was to learn later, they included managing directors, accountants, clerks, underwriters, stock-brokers and bank managers. Many of them had the typical reserve and stiff upper lip which I have come to associate with a certain class of Englishman. Not my cup of tea at all. I sighed heavily, but resigned myself to suffer the half-hour or so. I had been trapped by my own inquisitiveness.

There is an old English saying, 'Curiosity killed the cat'. In my case it did much more. The Rev Dick Lucas gave a short address in which he expounded clearly and simply the Christian gospel. My eyes were opened and my world turned upside down. My soul had reached flashpoint and from now on my life was to take on a new meaning and purpose. Suddenly and most unexpectedly, I had come to the end of my spiritual pilgrimage. Yet, paradoxically, the end was to prove a beginning, a beginning without an end, for beyond my understanding or deserving I had entered into eternal life.

2: In the melting pot

Mine had been a long journey. For its origin we have to go back thousands of years before I was born to a time 2000 years before the birth of Christ in Bethlehem. Abraham may not yet have been born. The proud city of London, where I still work, did not exist. In its place were swampy marshlands besides the Thames and drier gravel terraces where late New Stone Age families lived in circular huts of wattle and daub.

Parts of my own country, however, were a culture ahead. Away in the far north-west, in the Punjab, the land of the five rivers, the Bronze Age was already well-established. Here in the Indus Valley there was an advanced civilisation with flourishing brick-built cities which bore every evidence of careful town planning. Wheeled traffic used the streets which were laid out in parallel lines. There were potteries, shops, granaries, public baths and temples where nature gods were worshipped, the whole served by elaborate drainage works. It was a thriving and prosperous community.

But over the mountains the storm clouds were gathering. There, beyond the frontier, lay the wild mountainous country which we know as Afghanistan, remote, unknown, untamed. Although in recent years it has very slowly and reluctantly begun to come to terms with the modern world even today much of the country's life remains as it was during the times of the Indus civilisation. It is a fascinating land, wrapped in unfathomable mystery. And it is there, four thousand years ago, that events started which were to bring about the birth of Hinduism a religion which today commands the allegiance of over five hundred million people. Let us try to visualise the Afghan landscape at that time.

In some parts sandy plains stretch to the horizon. The wind, which is blowing clouds of yellow dust, has swept the surface into giant corrugations which make travelling a nightmare. Except by the occasional oases and streams the vegetation is sparse, consisting mainly of stunted scrub. All around are the mountains where the elements have carved the red sandstone rocks into fantastic shapes. Surely this must be the abomination of desolation, stark, elemental, scorched by the pitiless sun.

In this arid habitat we marvel that there is any animal life at all yet on the plains we see wild sheep, donkeys, Bactrian camels and gazelles, some pursued by wolves and leopards. Away in the distance, vultures are dropping, silent and sinister, on the body of a wild goat. Higher up the mountainside an ibex bounds away as a bear comes into view whilst on the snow line we hear the harsh calls of the snow-cocks.

The sound of human voices turns our gaze to a rough track where several herdsmen clothed in goatskins are shepherding a large flock of sheep. These are nomads, tall and fair with narrow heads. Their ancestors were wandering hunters and although they have long since learnt to domesticate sheep, they are nomads still, journeying each year over hundreds of miles of the most difficult terrain imaginable. They survive, but only just. Without a doubt the harsh surroundings have contributed to their toughness and fine physical stamina. Yet environment is only half the story. There is also heredity. In the light of subsequent events it seems certain that these men have inherited the fierce fighting instincts of their forbears.

How the great invasion began is a mystery but there is nothing to stop us making intelligent guesses. A year of famine may have driven them south-eastwards through the passes to seek a richer land. A sudden surge of fury may have overtaken these men of violence as they brooded in their goatskin tents. The Indus culture was contemporary with the great Sumerian civilisation in the Middle East and it would have been only too easy for the Asian tribesmen to learn from long-distance camel caravans of the rich cities beyond the mountains. Or maybe some of the more venturesome amongst them had, one year, travelled farther than any of their race had ever dared before and, like Joshua's spies at Jericho, had gazed with wondering eyes on a land flowing with milk and honey.

Whatever the reason, the time came when hordes of grim-faced warriors assembled together under their tribal chiefs to make the long, long trek into the Indus valley. Their weapons were probably a strange mixture, swords and spears of bronze, and stone bows which are still used in the remoter parts of Afghanistan today. Their flocks travelled with them in the care of the elderly and disabled. When, after many days' journeyings, they streamed through the mountain passes they found cities where the inhabitants had grown soft and decadent.

Victory was certain. Many of the dark-skinned Dravidians of the cities were massacred; not even children escaped the sword. Some, however, were able to flee in time and moved south-eastwards down on to the Deccan. A few who remained had their lives spared because as captives they could do useful work for the victors. So a thousand year old culture came to a violent end.

The next part of the story is obscure in many details but from archaeological discoveries and the ancient Hindu scriptures we can learn the main outlines. The Aryan invaders were relatively uncultured men besides the Dravidians. Not for them the delights of city life nor the scholar's leisured construction of picture writing. It comes as no surprise to us to learn that writing was abandoned for many a year – a long, sad step backwards into the barbarian past. The cities themselves were destroyed and without a doubt much of great architectural value was demolished.

Some mingling of the races, and consequent assimilation of practices and beliefs, inevitably took place although the subsequent development of the caste system must have put a severe brake on this. The Aryans' nomadic tendencies, so essential in the mountains but so unnecessary on an alluvial plain, gradually ceased as they settled, not in the ruined cities, but in a string of small villages.

Religious beliefs were also absorbed. The Dravidians believed in what is now called *Karma*, the moral law of cause and effect. They worshipped a mother goddess. This was a concept alien to the

Aryans who thought of God as father. Despite this, however, they accepted into their religion the natives' belief and henceforth thought of God as being both male and female. So today Hinduism has a number of female goddesses. Perhaps surprisingly to Western eyes, some of these goddesses are conceived of as cruel and vindictive; in paintings and in sculpture they are shown with blood dripping from their lips. Despite this, many Hindus today think of God as the Great Mother exemplifying all the finest maternal attributes.

The Aryan tribesmen also made their own distinctive contribution to the new religion. Central to their faith was the offering of animal sacrifices by means of which they believed that the creative process of life was continually being renewed.

For the growth of this new religion we turn to the next chapter.

3: At random

When I think about the origin of the religion of my fathers the story of the little slave girl in *Uncle Tom's Cabin* comes into my mind.

'Where were you born?'

'Never was born,' persisted Topsy.

'Do you know who made you?'

'Nobody as I knows on,' said the child with a short laugh . . . 'I 'spect I growed.'

Hinduism has no founder, no clear-cut beginning. Like Topsy, it just grew. The word is derived from the Persian word Hindostan which was the name given to the Indus valley by the Aryan tribesmen. An alternative term sometimes used is Brahminism. It is a very complex religion not easy either for a Westerner to comprehend or for a Hindu to explain. Perhaps we should regard its complexity as being quite properly in keeping with the multi-faceted diamond that is India.

The first obvious fact is that there is no creed. Apart from the various scriptures there is no doctrinal statement that a devout Hindu can use as a guideline to belief and conduct or that an interested enquirier can turn to for explanation. This accounts for much of our difficulty in describing this religion. It explains why a Hindu can more or less believe what he wants and still be considered true to his faith. It also is the reason why Indians in general are very tolerant of other world religions. Perhaps, too, it is at least indirectly the basis for the total absence of proselytising zeal. An earnest Christian cannot help but be an evangelist; he wants to share what he has found with others. A Hindu, on the other hand, has no such incentive because it is impossible for anyone not born into the faith to become a Hindu.

Hinduism is really a compound of religion, philosophy and a highly specialised social system. Within it there is tremendous variety of belief and conduct. Everything is continually evolving; even gods disappear, to be replaced by others. There is a constant state of flux.

The religious aspect involves worship of the gods in the highly ornamental temples for which India is famous. Offerings are a prominent feature of the temple worship and these are offered by the priests who are known as Brahmins. There is nothing in the temple, however, which in any way corresponds with a Christian service because Hindus do not practise corporate worship. They visit the temple simply as individuals concerned only with their own relationship with whatever god they are approaching. Their goal is to achieve union with the Ultimate Reality who lies behind the various gods. This state of blessedness is called *Moksha* and if there is a spiritual heart to Hinduism, this is it. The devout Hindu has a strong sense of his obligation to carry out religious duties and it is common practice to visit the temple daily. He also has a firmly-held belief in a moral law of cause and effect: that if he does wrong he will suffer.

There is a strand of philosophic mysticism in

Hinduism. The migration of souls is perhaps rather a strange doctrine to Western minds but Indians believe that after a lapse of time the soul returns to the earth to occupy another human body. This process of reincarnation may be repeated a number of times until *Moksha* is achieved.

The sacredness of all life is a noble concept which some Hindus carry to extreme lengths so that they regard treading upon an insect as sin. The cow is especially sacred and is allowed to go its way without let or hindrance. So in the villages cows can be seen lying in the road, indifferent to the swerving traffic. They eat vegetables in the bazaars before the anguished eyes of the stallholder and no one dares to say them nay. To eat beef would be blasphemy. Other sacred objects are certain species of trees, snakes, monkeys and of course the sacred river Ganges.

The material world is thought of as an illusion, giving a deceptive appearance of reality. Escape from the bondage of this world is something to be eagerly sought after. One way of escape is by the practice of yoga, discipline used as an aid to mystic contemplation. Mantras are mystic words used in yoga; they are spoken over and over again until the reciter goes into a semi-hypnotic state.

Hinduism has had a profound effect on the social life of India. There is not the separation between sacred and secular that occurs in some countries, for example, in Britain. The carefree jollifications at the festivals are joined in by all the community. Onlookers wear colourful costumes and images of some of the gods are carried in procession accompanied by gaily decorated elephants. These are great social occasions though they are essentially religious.

The same is true of the forms of classical dancing for which India is justly famous. Originating in the temple worship as an offering of praise to the gods the dances are composed of graceful movements of the human body, of facial expression, of singing and musical accompaniment. These are all elevated to a deeply sensitive, fine portrayal of religious art. Some of the dance dramas depict the human soul in search of God, the very search in which I was engaged myself. In my own State of Kerala the particular form of ritual dancing engaged in is known as *Kathakali* and it is a dramatic expression of two religious epics. The performance of these dramas used to last all night in the temples but in modern times a selective version now lasts only a couple of hours.

Rooted deep in Indian consciousness is the noble concept of non-violence though it is certainly not universally accepted in the country. Outside of India this tradition became known through the life and work of its greatest exponent, Mahatma Gandhi. With marked insight, some might say cunning, he developed the idea into a positive form of passive resistance which was called *yagraha*. This was sometimes used with great effect when the police attempted to break up protest demonstrations. With Gandhi's tragic and violent death and with independence achieved, this particular expression of Hinduism received a setback from which it has not recovered. But its roots, the sacredness of human life remain.

By far the most important influence of Hinduism on daily life in India has been the operation of the caste system. This is a believe of great antiquity. Like other aspects of Indian religion it has gradually evolved from a relatively simple concept into one which is exceedingly complex.

What, then, is a caste? Put simply it is a social group of people engaged in similar occupations, living a similar sort of life and bound together by traditional customs somewhat in the manner of the mediaeval craft guilds in England. The castes are graded in a pecking order and there are what, to the Westerner, seem incredibly rigid distinctions between them. Originally there were just three castes. The highest is that of the *Brahmins* all of whom belong to the priestly order and this fact itself is sufficient to stress the over-riding place of religion in the life of the Indian people. Next below them are the *Kshatryas* who are the warrior aristocrats; many today are government officials and the like. It is to this caste that I belong. The third consist of farmers, the *Vaishyas*. As agriculture developed this caste was divided into two. Landowners and farmers remained *Vaishyas* whilst farm workers and other labouring classes became *Shudras*. These are the four main castes into which every Indian, except those who are outcasts, is born. It is not possible for anyone to move into a higher caste in this life although the objective is to enter a higher one in a subsequent reincarnation. Marriage outside the caste is not allowed. Through the centuries innumerable sub-divisions of the castes have been created so that today there are about three thousand.

But one social group stands by itself in tragic isolation. These are the *Pariahs* or Untouchables of whom there are more than seventy million. They are sometimes known as outcasts and perform the most menial tasks in society. Caste members operate the most blatant discrimination against them, regarding them as unclean simply because they do the dirty though essential work of the community. It is to the eternal credit of Mahatma Gandhi that he, the pacifist, fought like a tiger by words and example on their behalf. In a deeply-moving phrase he attempted to lift their lowly status by insisting that they should be called not outcasts but *Harijans*, the people of God. As a result of his work they were eventually allowed to enter the temples. Recent legislation has banned some of the worst forms of discrimination against them.

Although Hinduism is not an historical revelation it has accumulated a number of sacred scriptures in which small fragments of ancient history are wrapped up in a mass of legend. Like parts of the Old Testament they were written hundreds of years after the events concerned. The words are in *Sanskrit*, a now dead language which was used in religious writing much in the same way as Latin is employed in the rituals of the Roman Catholic church. The books in their entirety are called *Vedas*, a word which means knowledge.

They are divided into three main groups. The first is the *Veda* proper, the contents of which were gathered together about 1200 BC making it one of the world's oldest religious books. It is divided into four sections. It begins with a collection of about a thousand, mainly very short, hymns and is followed by the priestly chants sung during the making of sacrifices. Next comes a litany of prayers and lastly a number of spells to be used in exorcisms.

The second group is known as the *Upanishads* and these are philosophical writings of a later date. They are concerned much more with mysticism and individual piety than with sacrificial rituals.

Finally of a later date still, is the *Bhagavadgita* consisting of two great religious epics. These are extremely popular with the ordinary people of India for they present religious truths in story form and are consequently comprehended more easily than the more esoteric writings.

So far the Westerner can express some sympathetic understanding of the tenets of Hinduism, even though he may not accept them. When we come to the many gods of this religion, and in particular to the images which portray them, it is a different story. Christians are at the very least taken aback by the grossly materialistic interpretations of God in a religion which professes to scorn materialism. They may well be appalled by the sheer number of gods. It has been jokingly said that there are as many gods as there are people in India. There are, in fact, about 33,000 gods which is an incredible number. Some of the gods have wives who are worshipped in their own right. Some are regarded as having a number of reincarnations which are called *avantars*. Some have different names and images according their differing moods. All in all, a complicated story. Since Hinduism is a religion which is constantly being added to, it is, I suppose, inevitable that the number of gods is going to build up too.

There are, however, three principal gods. *Brahma* is the creator, *Vishnu* the preserver and *Siva* the destroyer. *Brahma* is not now worshipped as much as formerly and is thought of as being impersonal but the other two still dominate the stage. *Vishnu* is one of the gods who has had a number of reincarnations, two of which, *Rama* and *Krishna*, are very popular. *Vishnu* and his manifestations are kindly gods. *Siva* is a god with a violent and unpredictable temper who has to be placated with sacrifices. His wife is the most important goddess and is known by several different names according to various aspects of her character. People may worship any god at all, and as many gods as they wish, but particular districts tend to have their favourite god or gods. Yet, paradoxically, Hinduism at its best, whilst cheerfully accepting many gods, recognises only one ultimate Being behind them all.

You will probably now have realised that there is immense variety, even contradictions within Hinduism. For example, the sacredness of all forms of life is inherent in this religion yet although there are Hindus who would carefully step aside to avoid treading on a beetle there are other equally devout adherents who become soldiers. There are vegetarians and there are meat eaters. Ritual and sacrifice are important to many Hindus but increasingly in these days there are others to whom ritualism is unacceptable and who concentrate instead on personal piety. To some, the religious life consists of strict denial of worldly pleasures and comforts – we see an extreme form of this in the fakir on his bed of nails. Others can see nothing in their religion which prevents them living a life of sensual indulgence. What we in Britain term the 'permissive society' is by no means unknown in India. Whilst the caste system has been an integral part of Hinduism from the very beginning, for a considerable time now there have been reform movements seeking to abolish caste altogether.

So, it is not that far wide of the mark to say that a practising Hindu can virtually believe what he likes! Such is the tolerance, or, as some might say, the vagueness, of modern Hinduism.

4: Boyhood days

It was the early morning hours of 21st August, 1930. In one of the bedrooms of Kundavalappil House there was an air of barely suppressed excitement. One of a small group of women held a motionless body suspended from her arm. A couple of vigorous slaps galvanised the silent form into protesting cries which were answered by the loud squawking of a crow in a jack-fruit tree outside the window. Yet one more human statistic had been added to India's teeming millions; I had arrived on planet earth.

If I had been given the choice, I could hardly have chosen a more delightful spot. Tourists and inhabitants alike describe Kerala as paradise. The coast consists of beautiful sandy beaches backed by blue lagoons interspersed with dunes supporting coconut palms. But my birthplace was some fifteen miles inland in the little village of Puzhakkal where there is beauty of a different kind. The name means 'village on the banks of the river'. Because of this river there is luxuriant vegetation which makes the area beautiful. The village is engulfed by a great emerald green sea of paddy fields which sweeps past the houses farther than the eye can see. There are also fields of fruit and vegetables and the road to the nearby town is fringed with trees.

Kunduvalappil House, my mother's home, is set back from the road in two acres of grounds. I remember ten types of banana trees as well as two especially large jack-fruit trees and many other trees and vegetables.

There was only one other house in the village of the size of my mother's home; most of the others were huts, not more than two dozen in all, occupied mainly by Roman Catholic labourers and Hindu outcasts who were untouchables. Other buildings were few indeed and all very small. There was a toddy shop and a liquor shop. Toddy is an alcoholic drink made from the buds of coconut trees. It is sold, together with boiled potatoes and other roots, in conditions which caste Hindus regard as totally unacceptable. Liquor shops sell the more expensive and powerful Indian-made gin. These are usually neat and clean places patronised by more sophisticated men. No ladies visited either type of place. Since devout male Hindus also eschew alcohol it was mainly Christians who visited the liquor shops and untouchables the toddy halls. Other buildings were two restaurants and a grocery store with the local library, such as it was, in a room above.

This idyllic rural locality was to be my home for only ten months. After this I was brought up in my father's home in the nearby town of Trichur while my mother remained at her home in Puzhakkal. In the villages in India after a wedding the bride usually returns to her mother's home and the husband likewise to his mother's home, visiting his wife's home at night if his work is in her locality. Normally the children grow up with the mother. I was an exception, however, for my father's household was short of

25

males and that was a serious matter. Men not only do the harder physical work but are responsible for the supervision and organisation of what are often very large households. Since my father worked morning, afternoon and evening six days a week there was need for a male who would at least have a little more time for housework than he did. So my change of home at the age of ten months was a case of long term planning!

My new abode, was only about three and a half miles from Puzhakkal village but its urban environment was very different from the rural surroundings of my mother's home. Trichur serves as a transport centre for a considerable area around it. From here buses travel north, south, east and west. There are also two railway stations.

The house in which we lived was a large one. It had to be to accommodate our extended family. It was two storeys high and built of mud and brick with a clay tile roof. As is common in Kerala a large open verandah went the whole front of the house. Indoors the furniture consisted of hard wooden benches and tables. There were neither cushions, carpets nor curtains. The lighting was electric but the cooking was done on an open wood fire. The floors were tiled and kept scrupulously clean; the twice-daily scrubbing by the servants was almost a ritual. There was half an acre of garden in which grew fruit and vegetables. The few flowers were cultivated for religious purposes.

I was looked after by one of my father's sisters. The household consisted of my father, his sisters and nieces, several women servants and myself. Except for one of my father's sisters who was a teacher, the entire family depended for their existence on my father's earnings. One of his sisters had been married to an editor of a famous Indian newspaper who died of heart failure. As was the legal custom, his own family took his money, leaving nothing for his wife and children, and my father was forced to support all six of them out of his meagre wages until they got married. In consequence he had to work very hard. Up to five o'clock in the evening he worked as a clerk in the Education Department. Then he came home for a hasty meal before going to the local Co-operative Society where he had another job which kept him busy until nine-thirty at night. So you see he had very little spare time for recreation, or for that matter, for managing household affairs.

Yet he always made time for his devotions, retiring morning and evening to the special room in the house which was kept exclusively as a shrine. Here he spent at least one hour in the morning and one and a half hours in the evening. This intensity of religious belief and conduct undoubtedly had a great effect on my impressionable mind.

I was the only boy in the house among many girls and there was no question but that the women of the household spoilt me. Very early in my life I was allowed and encouraged to exercise powers of leadership and organisation.

The local infants' school took entrants at the age of five but my father was anxious for me to begin my education and special permission was obtained for me to start school some three months early.

Because of the intense heat the main school holiday lasts for two months during April and May so I began my scholastic career at the beginning of June.

The buildings were just half a mile from my home and my twenty year old male cousin took me the first day. Like many a boy in many a country the whole idea was strange and unacceptable; I cried my heart out. After that first day I was left to my own devices. The way to school led over a railway crossing and sometimes I used to stop and watch the trains passing. At that early age they were objects of mystery to me. Gigantic machines that thundered along the rails – where did they come from and where did they go? Perhaps it was these moments which sowed the seeds of my later delight in travel.

This was on the way home from school; I would not have dared to dawdle on the way there. The lady teachers were quite strict and although we were only infants they were not slow to use the cane on us. This in any case was a type of punishment with which I was already familiar. My father had a fiery temper and although he did not beat me more than perhaps twice a year, when he did he made it an occasion to remember. I had only been attending infants' school for a few weeks when a few rough boys wrote some words on the walls of the school toilets. The words intrigued me although in my innocence I did not know what they meant. I thought it would be a splendid idea to show off my writing prowess by reproducing them in the toilet at home. My scandalised household, alas, thought otherwise. When accused I tried to take the easy way out and vehemently denied being the culprit. My father, however, was having none of that for my handwriting gave me away. My lies had only made matters worse in his eyes and a severe whipping followed.

The effect of this comparatively trivial incident

was that I became more skilful at lying my way out of scrapes. Perhaps if someone had only taken the trouble to explain to a little boy that the words were obscene I would have found truthfulness more attractive. Punishment, at any rate, did not stop me from being naughty. The time of going home from school coincided with the time that the cows were brought in from grazing in the forest. There were a considerable number of these cows and the boys who accompanied them were two or three hundred yards away behind the herd. It was always the custom to carry umbrellas as protection from the heat and these umbrellas had other uses. When a ferocious cow came by it was a great delight to open the umbrella as quick as a flash in the animal's face and then to step back hastily. We used to laugh uproariously as the terror-stricken beast ran full pelt down the street. You should have seen the chaos that followed – the confusion amongst the other cows, the panic of the men and women in the direct path of the animal as they scrambled to safety, the frightened faces of the passers-by. We, of course, walked away innocent as angels.

For the four years that I was at this school I was, I suppose, an average pupil but I did not learn as much as I ought; this was not because the subjects were beyond me but simply because I was lazy. How I have regretted that laziness since, especially when I have had examinations to take.

At the age of eight I transferred to St Thomas' High School which was a Roman Catholic establishment though by no means all of the teachers were Catholics; a number were Hindus including some Brahmins. There was no attempt on the part of the

Catholics to proselytise; indeed if there had my father would have been angry and would certainly have insisted on my having a ceremonial bath to purify me from Christian contamination! But he knew St Thomas' was a good school and so long as his son received a good education he did not mind if the teachers were Roman Catholic.

School did not even begin with an assembly but the Christian boys were forced to stop behind when school finished in order to learn the catechism. I did not know what this was but anything that kept you at school could not be good and I was glad that I was not a Christian.

The headmaster was a Roman Catholic priest, Father Kallingal. He was a holy terror. Determined to maintain discipline at all cost he caned everyone; yet he was an affectionate man and I know that he liked me.

This school was more than three miles from my father's home and I had to walk there barefoot. In fact, I never wore any kind of shoes until I was sixteen years old. Sometimes I used to wear a shirt and shorts but often I wore the traditional 'lungi' which is a cloth like a towel some three yards long wrapped round the body.

Each day began at six o'clock with a bath or shower; sometimes I used to go to the nearest pond for a bathe. When this was done I would set off walking to the temple for my devotions. Religion to me was as much a part of life as the washing which preceded it; indeed, this personal cleansing was essentially a religious activity. On returning home my devotions were rewarded with a cup of tea made with a little milk and unpurified sugar. This sugar actually had a horrible taste but I wonder if you will understand me when I tell you that because I was so hungry, it was lovely. Then I got down to my school homework until nine o'clock when we had our breakfast, such as it was. It never varied and consisted of a little rice and curry.

Fifteen minutes later I had started on my three mile walk to school. Sometimes on my way to school I would catch sight of a large snake slithering through the vegetation and instinctively I avoided it for I was well aware of the possible dangers. The school was too far away for me to walk home for the midday meal. This in any case, was a luxury we could not afford. So when I returned home in the afternoon I was ravenously hungry.

I usually had a cup of tea and sometimes, if I was lucky, a little rice as well. A little bit of studying followed but most of the evening was spent in doing housework. One of my more enjoyable tasks was collecting coconuts which were used in curries and I revelled in shinning up the trunks of the tall palms. Not all of my duties were as pleasant as that but in the main I did not find the tasks too disagreeable since my responsibility as household organiser gave me an opportunity to throw my weight around.

At dusk the entire family gathered for what we called 'puja' in the room set aside as a shrine. 'Puja' means prayer performed in front of the image of a god. We had a number of photographs of various gods and in general worshipped them indiscriminately. If my father had a favourite, it was undoubtedly Krishna. He was one of the incarnations of Vishnu and was always the object of much devotion in Kerala.

For these devotions we never knelt down but squatted on the floor and folded our hands. The prayers consisted of rapid recitation of mantras in Sanskrit, the ancient language of the Hindu scriptures. We sang hymns which extolled the greatness of God. If we had recently come into contact with an untouchable we had to bathe in a loin cloth before going to the temple and then had to remain in the wet cloth to pray. This, of course, was not very pleasant but it certainly made sure that I did not fall asleep!

Then came the main meal of the day, a dish of rice and curry. This will probably seem to you a very monotonous diet and so indeed it was, even though various kinds of curry were made, but when you are hungry you are only too glad to eat anything that is going and variety of fare was an undreamt of luxury. We did not pray before meals and the custom of saying grace was completely foreign to us. In fact, surprisingly enough, there is no word for 'thank-you' in India. We say instead, 'It has been helpful', 'Very nice', 'It is good'. After the meal was over I did some more study and then went to sleep.

Studies and work at home left very little leisure time. A traditional Indian game is called carram and I did occasionally play this with another boy. The board on which it is played is three feet square with a hole in each corner. The twenty-four counters used are black and white, similar to draughts. The object is to get as many of the counters as possible into the holes. During the holidays I played cricket and football and for a short while, hockey.

There was no money in the family for expensive luxuries like toys. In any case, it was not the custom to have many toys in Kerala. The commonest used by school children was the top made of wood with a nail and string but I did not even have this amusement. Occasionally, on days of great excitement, relatives arrived from distant parts bearing largesse which included toys. These were, however, bittersweet times for me. The toys were duly unwrapped from their parcels, shown to me, even placed in my hands for a short while, and then taken away from my wistful eyes to be placed in a glass case where they seemed almost to acquire a religious significance for they were proudly displayed at festival times.

Despite the seriousness, almost solemnity, of my daily life I was happy except for one fact; I had a most unsatisfactory relationship with my father. I am sure now that he loved me but he never showed it. He never took me in his arms or talked affectionately to me. He spoke to other members of the family but not to me. As a consequence I developed an intense dislike of him and would go to extreme lengths to avoid having to meet him in the house or garden. It was probably something lacking in his emotional make-up which prevented him from expressing love. Many a time during the school holidays I saw my mother deeply depressed and crying because my father visited her so seldom.

In the school holidays I went to live with my mother and her relatives. Holidays were Heaven. I revelled in the natural beauty of the countryside – the river, the trees and the fields full of lush crops.

My mother and I inevitably did not have a very close relationship because we saw each other so seldom but I know she loved me very much. Like my father she was a stern disciplinarian and punished me quite often which did nothing to improve our relationship. So I grew up not experiencing parental love and companionship as it is known in the West. I do not, however, wish to depict my mother as a tyrant. She was very God-fearing, humble, innocent and, despite her strictness, fairly easy to get along with. Although she was not very bright she worked hard and was cleverer than her sisters who lived with her.

It was a pleasant change for me to have a break from household responsibilities. Since in the main eight week holiday in April and May the weather was always extremely hot a favourite pastime of mine was to go to the river where I used to bathe and splash around to my heart's content. Sometimes I would get into a punt and pole myself down the river disturbing the brightly-coloured kingfishers from the bankside vegetation.

It was during this main holiday that Pooram, the greatest of all the Hindu festivals, took place. It is focussed on the Vadakkunathan temple in Trichur. This is the largest of over twenty temples in the town and is dedicated to Siva. Its walls are so thick that they accommodate rooms between the inner and outer skins. Around the inner shrine are elaborate carvings of sexual acts with paintings of gods below. The temple itself is in a dominating position on an elevated open space which has a three mile circular road around its perimeter. Altogether, a superb site for the great religious festivals.

These were occasions of much excitement to me. Remember I had no toys, seldom played games and never went to the seaside for a holiday; the festivals served as substitutes for all these and they really are wonderful. The Pooram at Trichur is the biggest in

Kerala and I was one of many people who were actively involved in it. A month beforehand I used to go from house to house collecting money with which to purchase the elaborate fireworks on which two thousand rupees were spent. That is an awful lot of money for a small Indian town to spend in such short-lived extravagance. But this is not only a much needed diversion from the monotonous grind of heavy toil, it is basically also a vehicle for the expression of intense religious emotions.

There is a double column of elephants with fifteen in each side. Each animal is bedizened with gold-plated cloth in the shape of a gigantic heart. Umbrellas are carried on top of the elephants and on the back of one of them the temple deity is transported. There is a morning procession and a much longer one in the afternoon which lasts beyond nightfall. How proud I was to march in the processions to the accompaniment of characteristic Indian music on a variety of instruments especially drums! When darkness descended the brilliant pyrotechnic display began and lasted all night. The erupting stars soared upwards into the velvety blackness of the night informing the people of the countryside for miles around that the Hindus of Trichur were exalting their gods.

Another religious activity in Hinduism is the pilgrimage. Travel was a rare event for us. It was not until after I had left home that my father was able to achieve what is the goal of every devout Hindu, a trip to the sacred river Ganges at Benares. But whilst I was still a boy my father, his sister and I did make a pilgrimage which, although it was a much shorter one, was nevertheless an enormous adventure for us. We travelled by train to the southern tip of India near

Cape Comorin where I watched the simultaneous setting of the sun and rising of the moon. The railway carriages were bone-shakers; the food was bad; the hotels were terrible. Our thirst was intense for there was very little water available and we did not take a water carrier with us. Yet on the whole we enjoyed our trip because we were trying to please God. I loved travelling to these new places and visiting the temples.

Temples fascinated me. Once every few weeks we used to attend a large temple dedicated to Krishna which was situated twenty miles away at Guruvarour. Sometimes we spent the whole weekend there. My father used to do voluntary work at a Trichur temple and from the age of ten years I became his assistant there. This was one of the ways that my religious life developed. There is in Hinduism nothing which equates with Christian Sunday schools, neither did my father instruct me in Hindu beliefs because it is not an authoritative religion. I learnt about my religion indirectly by observation, by reading the scriptures daily at home, and by listening to the story-tellers in the temple as they recounted the great religious epics. Only young members of the Brahmin caste are taught the mantras by heart and the high philosophical teaching of Hinduism is acquired by less than 0.2 per cent of the population.

The temple where I did the voluntary work was Thiruvambadi which was dedicated to Krishna. It was situated at a road junction less than a quarter of a mile from my home. The entrance to the temple was a massive carved gate in the South Indian style with rooms built into it. Behind the huge outside wall was a concrete path circling the inner temple on which people walked round and round to please God. I often did seven rounds daily, bowing each time I came in front of the shrine entrance. We had to take our shirts and slippers off before passing through the outside gate and were only permitted in the inner temple if we had had a bath of purification. Only the priest could enter into the two innermost, pagoda-like shrines. The inner temple contained many oil lamps and it was one of my jobs to light these on special occasions such as worshippers' birthdays. Often in the evenings a storyteller would give the epics in great dramatic style. I used to sit down and listen enthralled.

Much of my temple work was in connection with the festivals. I helped my father in such matters as looking after the paid musicians, arranging for their food and sleeping quarters. We used to engage in a none too friendly rivalry with a neighbouring temple to hire the tallest elephants. This competition and all the other activity of temple worship seems very childish to me now that I am a Christian. Kerala was my home but now I am a Christian I feel like a stranger in the world knowing that here 'I have no abiding city', and I am no longer on the same wavelength as Hinduism.

Through my work in the temple I became quite well-known in the town and gained a reputation for being helpful. There was another way that I became a familiar figure to the people of Trichur and that was by the assistance I gave to my father in his political canvassing. Kerala has long been a very politically conscious part of India. When the nation gained independence the average literacy rate taken over the country as a whole was thirteen per cent whilst parts of what is now Kerala had achieved ninety-six per cent. My father supported the Congress candidates and he and I used to work very hard at door to door visitation and the distribution of leaflets. My boyish heart swelled with pride as I discovered that the politicians we supported always seemed to win.

As I look back on my childhood I realise now what a hard life my father endured. He worked himself to the point of exhaustion in order to maintain his large, extended family. But not content with that, his social and religious consciousness drove him to the voluntary work I have just described. In a land where bribery and corruption were commonplace his integrity shone out like a beacon. One small incident will illustrate this. One day when I was fifteen years old he sent me to the bank to collect a hundred rupees. The clerk gave me a hundred and twenty by mistake and I realised this as soon as I had checked the money. For a moment I hesitated but quickly I made up my mind to leave the matter for my father to decide. When I arrived home and gave my explanation my father was very cross and immediately made me walk the three miles back to the bank to return the surplus money. If this had happened in England it would not have been anything out of the way, thank God, but in India it was quite remarkable.

5: In ambition's clutches

Like, I suppose, many another youngster I began to develop a mixture of ambitions in my later school days. I wanted to marry a beautiful girl, have a successful business career and thirdly, what every devout Hindu youth desires, to seek God. I should perhaps explain that Hindus are always seeking God but do not expect to find him until they die. Years later, all of my ambitions were to be realised but in ways that I could not possibly have imagined whilst I was a boy.

In 1941 when I was eleven years old a world event took place which indirectly was to influence my life through my marriage. The Japanese invaded Burma. It so happened that one of my father's nieces was married to an officer stationed at the Indian embassy in Rangoon. They had been there a few years and were enjoying a happy life with their three daughters. Although the Second World War was under way, in Burma they felt safe and life was virtually normal.

Then one morning in 1941 some planes appeared unexpectedly above the city and bombs rained down. Pandemonium and chaos followed for the authorities were unprepared for this and great damage was caused. There were indescribably terrible scenes; at a stroke life had changed from happiness to misery. The embassy was ordered to be closed and the families of the staff, including my father's niece with her children, boarded the last passenger ship for India. They naturally arrived at Trichur, to my great delight. Living under the same roof with my relations who had been abroad and succeeded well added fuel to my ambition to travel and do something great in life.

The men remained behind to look after, as best they could, the Embassy documents and possessions. Nearly all of these possessions had to be abandoned when they were directed to retreat in successive stages to the northern region. Japanese troops had by this time invaded Burma and the inhabitants feared for their lives. Eventually the Embassy staff were left to escape back to India as best they could on foot. These administrators were, in the main, men who had lived a fairly sheltered existence in their beautiful homes with big cars and a luxurious standard of living. Some had done hardly any walking in their life but all had to negotiate without proper food or water the harsh, inhospitable terrain of jungle and mountain which marks the boundary between India and Burma. In typical Hindu fashion their thoughts were concentrated, not on the magnificent scenery, but on the deep, underlying philosophical problems of their tribulations. Why did they have to suffer like this? Of what were they guilty? When would the punishments of the Almighty cease and his favour be restored to them? These were ultimate questions that were far easier to ask than to answer. The only conclusion they could come to was that a person should adjust himself to his fate since what was destined could not be altered and God's will must have its way.

As they journeyed they were forced to shed more and more of their possessions, even clothing, because they were not strong enough to carry them. In the jungle they had to ward off attacks by wild animals. Many of the evacuees dropped dead of exhaustion and starvation. Eventually, after experiencing the horrors of hell, those who were left reached the town of Impala from where, after rest, they returned to their own localities by train. So one of them in due course reached our home and rejoined his wife and family, not forgetting, especially not forgetting, his most beautiful baby daughter Susheila.

Meanwhile my school studies took an increasing amount of my time. The boys who came top in the class always had family help at home. In my case I was left to myself except for an occasional exhortation to study and warning that when I grew up I would be good for nothing except to carry tiffin for other more successful boys. Tiffin is the meal sent at midday in a lunch box to the office or school. So the average measure of success which I achieved was due to my own determination and hard work.

Having lived all her young life in Burma, Susheila's eldest sister found it difficult to adjust to the mother tongue of Kerala state which is Malayalam. She was therefore admitted to a convent school two years lower in standard than my class though she was only three months younger than I. We became closer than a brother and sister and this, in a way, altered the course of my life. Having to teach someone else gave me a good grounding in mathematics and laid the foundation of an ability to communicate, in simple practical terms, truths that are otherwise difficult to comprehend. I did not know at that time that little events like these and the difficult times I had to go through were going to have a profound effect on my future life and that God was training and guiding me.

At school I prepared myself for the school-leaving certificate which is the equivalent of G.C.E. or O.N.C., in England. I took this when I was fourteen years old, having obtained special permission to take it early. I chose my favourite subject mathematics, then physics, chemistry, history, geography, Malayalam and English. It was necessary to pass all; if you failed in one you failed the lot and I failed in English. The effect on me was devastating. I knew that I had come to a crisis point, my whole life was at a standstill. How bitterly I regretted not applying my mind more assiduously to my studies when I was younger. Admission to an engineering degree had become virtually impossible and my ambition lay smashed into bits before me.

In desperation I prayed to God. It was an entirely different kind of prayer from those I normally prayed each day. Up to that moment my relationship with God had been based on family practice and the tradition of my race. I could see in the world of Nature evidence of a creator; I could not help but believe in God. But it was very much a formal affair. Now for the first time in my life I turned to God in a personal way.

'Lord, help me through this situation. Lead and direct my life from now on and I promise you I will follow. I have made a mess of my life and I have failed. You are my only help now.'

Tears rolled down my cheeks as I listened to various relatives of mine discussing with my father the sad state of my situation and the bleak prospect of my future life. I threw myself into the hands of God. A few weeks later a second result came through from Madras University. With trembling hands I perused the document then let out a cry of delight. I had passed! It was unbelievable; it had never happened before. And I had not even specifically prayed to God for this. It was beyond even the imagination of my wildest dreams.

This was not only an important stepping stone towards the career I had chosen but it was also a turning point in my religious life. I knew the reality of God not only because of his works in creation but because he had answered my prayer. I developed a greater confidence that my ambitions would succeed despite my poverty because I felt sure that God was with me. I prayed in a different sense, in a more personal way, from that time onwards. As I look back now I can see how God was gently guiding me.

Of course, my understanding of God was still that of a Hindu. I wanted nothing to do with Christianity and understood nothing about it despite being brought up in a Roman Catholic high school. I did not know the difference between Roman Catholicism and Protestantism and such was my ignorance that I thought that the Anglican Church Missionary Society was another religion! The Indians who were Roman Catholics did not impress me favourably at all. They still retained the caste system and consulted horoscopes in the pagan manner. They seemed to me to be less spiritual than Hindus and without a sense of holiness.

In the grounds of the high school was a separate establishment which was one of the outlying colleges of Madras University. Here I was to spend the next two years of my life in preparatory study for a degree. I formed a close friendship with another Hindu. We played tennis together, shared the preparations of our homework and had endless discussions on religion.

I remember saying to him one day, 'You're going to be a doctor when you finish at the University and I'm going to be an engineer. When we leave the college we may never meet again so let's make an agreement. If you die first you come and tell me what's up there in heaven or if I die first I'll communicate somehow what happened when I died and whether there is a God or not.'

This little pact shows the immaturity of my beliefs. My confidence that I could communicate at random after death was an indication both of an ill-informed attitude and an unwarranted cocksureness on my part. The doubts about the existence of God show that I was not as positive in my faith as I had thought I was. Because I was brought up in a God-fearing family I had some kind of peace and trust in God that he was guiding me daily and channelling my desires. Although that peace and trust were different from what I have now they were better than nothing because they kept me seeking God and being useful to others. So I had some kind of happiness. I know from my own life that one does not have to be a Christian to have an experience of God: the kind of experience one has when prayers are answered or when one looks at a colourful butterfly or flower, or at a breathtakingly beautiful sunset and

44

meditates on God's creation with a praising heart. But that is different from finding God today in this life.

It was during my university days that one of my uncles invited me to spend a day on board his ship. My mother had five brothers, four of whom worked on ships, and this one was captain of his. To me, for a boy in his early teens, that journey in a big steam-engined train towards ships which had sailed the oceans was an adventure packed with excitements. To add delight to my first independent trip into the outside world the fifty miles of my journey took me through the beautiful valleys of picturesque Kerala with their lush vegetation, thatched cottages and rippling streams all set against a backcloth of mountains.

As the train puffed slowly along birds in the nearby trees sang sweet melodies to the ambitious, adventurous boy inside who wondered whether he was travelling through a fairyland. The buffalos bathing in the rivers lifted their heads from the water, shaking them up and down in nods of approval. The elephants on the opposite bank lifted their trunks to blow fountains of water as though in celebration of my journey. The tall elegant coconut trees with their outstretched palm leaves appeared to be clapping their hands in the wind as a sign that they, too, shared my happiness. The mango and jackfruit trees, their luscious fruit-filled branches stretching up to the skies, lined the route in full decoration. Banana and betel nut trees waved at me to wish me good luck.

As the train approached Cochin harbour I could see numerous fishermen's nets in the bay poised over the water on tall bamboo frames ready to pounce on unsuspecting, passing shoals of fish. With what a thrill I walked up the gangway that day! How enjoyable it was to roam the ship, chatting to the officers and seamen. How exciting it was to look at nearby ships tied up to buoys, all busy loading or discharging cargos. My eager young eyes took in every detail. I wished there were more hours to the day. As I toured the ship from bow to stern learning how each section functioned I was fascinated by the engine room where I had a long conversation with the chief engineer officer. That was just the sort of practical life for me. I made up my mind: I would be a marine engineer.

I passed the Inter B.Sc. exam first time, getting a distinction in maths. My ambition was now firmly focussed on the sea and I was impatient to get there. I knew that because of my family's poverty a degree in engineering would be beyond my reach but I remembered from my earlier conversation with the engineer officer on my uncle's ship that it was possible to become a marine engineer after practical training in workshops. If I could get a job I would be able to travel round the world at no expense to myself and get paid for it. Marvellous! I decided to go to Bombay. The problem of getting there was soon solved. My mother's eldest brother, whom I knew as 'Big Uncle', was a purser. He was able to take me on board his ship from Cochin to Bombay. He had a heart of gold and a great affection for me and did a lot to help me get on in engineering.

So in August 1947 I sailed to Bombay. Arrangements had been made for me to stay initially with one of my father's nieces; later on I moved into lodgings.

My word, what an eye-opener it was for me, just seventeen years old, to go to this great maritime city from the little provincial town of Trichur. Bombay was a strange mixture of old and new. There were modern, many-storied hotels and ancient hovels; the latest cars and horse-drawn carriages called Victorias. Even in my lodgings, life was different for I had to fend for myself. There were no servants now and I had to do my own cooking and laundry.

Shortly after my arrival my other uncle who was a captain brought his ship into Bombay for a refit. He, too, was very anxious to help me and he sought and obtained permission from the owners for me to work in the engine room without pay. So I started work in September and for three months I laboured each day from eight o'clock in the morning to five o'clock in the evening. Although I received no money I gained a very useful amount of practical knowledge.

The ship was berthed in Mazagon Dock which was the workshop for the P. & O. and British India shipping lines. The head of the fitting shop was a Scotsman, Mr. O. A. Anderson. He was a very influential man who was effectively assistant to the general works manager and during the refit my uncle got to know him quite well. It was now a matter of some urgency for me to get a formal apprenticeship as a marine engineer. I tried for several jobs without success.

The Mazagon Dock company itself took four engineer apprentices each year. Eagerly I applied for one of these apprenticeships but my heart sank when I learnt that there were a hundred and nineteen other applicants. From these a short list was compiled of thirty who were to be called for a written exam. In the main these young men came from influential families in Bombay, sons of well-to-do merchants and Government officials. I was fortunate indeed to be included but the reason for this was because the foreman was on friendly terms with my uncle and knew him to be honest and hardworking so I was given a chance for his sake.

But the letter of invitation was never sent. In India these things happen. Perhaps someone wanted to substitute another applicant. Fortunately my uncle had been informed that I was on the short list so I went to the exam despite the lack of a written invitation. In the event, I was selected as one of the four successful candidates. The foreman told my uncle how well I had answered the difficult questions. It was not that I was any cleverer but God gives wisdom to those who seek him diligently and fear him. One or two of the questions were rather tricky but God opened my eyes to the hidden catches. Along with my interest in mathematics the experience God had given me on the ship served me in good stead and I coped satisfactorily.

So far, so good. Having been accepted for one of the posts I next had to have a medical. The doctor who examined me lost no time in disqualifying me for being under age. At that time I was rather small for my age, 'Four foot six and nothing', and I had lived a sheltered and morally pure life. I had to fight hard to get in, telling him of my ten years at school and of my subsequent university exam, the certificates of which I had to produce. In the end God over-ruled and I was accepted.

On the evening before I was due to start work at Mazagon Dock, Mahatma Gandhi was assassinated.

What a sad day that was for India. The next day was proclaimed a national day of mourning and all work ceased so I began my working life twenty-four hours later than expected.

My period in the workshop was quite successful. I was so eager to gain knowledge that most days I worked hard, up to nine o'clock at night, with no overtime wages. Many of the other apprentices gave a high priority to sport, especially hockey, and did the minimum of work. I must have seemed like a wet blanket to them for I never joined in any of their games, work being all-important to me. I was determined to succeed. As a consequence I was, as you might imagine, very popular with the fitters and turners. The financial reward for my industry, however, was sparse indeed. My daily wage was half a rupee which is equivalent to about 3p. My uncle had to give me a little extra money monthly to keep me going. My income went up a little each year but even at the end of my apprenticeship it was still barely at subsistence level. Every Saturday I went to the Victoria Jubilee Technical Institute doing part-time studies for four years. Each year I came top and on the completion of the course I was awarded a bronze medal for achieving the highest marks. When the examination time came along I found that three hours had been allotted for the maths paper but in half an hour I had answered all the questions and left the room. The reason for my speed was two-fold. I had done every sum in the book thoroughly even before the class lecture was given and so had all the sums at my fingertips and, equally important, I loved maths.

I had reached a stage of my career where the hard

graft of study lay behind me and work became a delight. I began to shine in engineering and coming top in all the practical engineering tests, I was a favourite with the foremen. Yet I found it much harder to grow in the spiritual life and in thoughtful moments I was conscious of, shall we say, imperfections. One of my besetting failures, for example, was a bad temper which I could not control. I recall that one day during my apprenticeship I was given a B.C.G. injection which made my arm a little tender. Later that day in the blacksmith's shop a fellow apprentice came up to me in a friendly manner and put his arm genially on mine. My temper flared up and I hit out at him with a pair of burning tongs which I was working with. If that was my response to friendliness you may well imagine my reaction to hostility! My workmates, I am ashamed to say, soon realised the need to treat their quick-tempered colleague with considerable circumspection. This bad trait of mine was to plague me for a number of years until my conversion to the Chrstian faith when it disappeared as God worked out his will daily in my life.

After I had been at Mazagon Docks about two years I returned to Trichur on a month's leave. What a homecoming that was – a very emotional time for the family as well as for myself. I had a feeling that I was coming home after years of absence. My heart burned with joy as I saw the countryside where I had grown up. Kerala was my homeland and I had a deep, deep love for the place. I felt that it was my home for eternity and I considered myself fortunate indeed to be one of its citizens.

Everybody was at the railway station to welcome

me. It seemed as though I had been away for many years. The roads and buildings looked different, scaled down, after two years of big city life. I was home at last and my immediate feelings urged me to stay put and never leave again. I walked through all the old, familiar places of my childhood and visited many of my relations. I was nineteen years old and felt a very important man. My brothers were glad to see me. They bore no resentment at my success. We were very, very close to each other and had mutual respect and love. I was treated like a king by the whole family, given the best food and followed wherever I went. All my relatives were delighted at the thought of my exciting engineering prospects and were proud of the future Chief Engineer.

Their pride re-activated my own ambition which the nostalgia of homecoming had temporarily blunted. As the month all too quickly came to an end I knew that I had to return to Bombay. But, oh, the anguish of parting, the hugging and the sobbing. It was as though I were leaving for ever to a foreign land. Bombay was only six hundred miles away as the crow flies but the train traversed fifteen hundred miles in its three day journey.

At the end of my apprenticeship Mr Anderson helped me to obtain a post as junior engineer with Mogul Lines. It was very difficult to get work on ships but because of the strong recommendation from the foreman I was accepted. But again I had to have a medical and again I was disqualified, this time because of a heart murmur which the doctor said made me unfit for work. I could not accept this and demanded a second opinion. The heart specialist examined me and after consulting with the first doctor said I could be accepted provided that I took some pills which he prescribed. I never took them and did not come to any harm.

So I started work as the 5th engineer on S.S. Alavi, a coal-burning ship. Once more I felt that God was protecting me and guiding my life. Starting a new job provided a powerful incentive to my already strong ambitions and I was determined to do well in the engine-room. I did not realise it at the time but of course I had got things the wrong way round. Ambition was in the driving seat and I expected God to help me fulfil my aims. It was putting the cart before the horse. I was still a Hindu and knew no better but it must be said that many a Christian is liable to fall into this error as well.

Life on board ship is tough for a raw recruit, especially for someone like myself, sensitive and timid and from a very sheltered Hindu home. Young officers are regarded as legitimate objects of merciless mickey-taking. I was particularly scared of one of the officers who drank like a fish. This man made such constant verbal attacks on me that one day I was driven to retaliation. I dramatically drew a knife from my pocket and threw it with a clatter on the table.

'The next one who makes remarks like that will get this stuck into them,' was my defiant challenge.

Of course, I did not really mean it for I was a peace-loving youth but everyone has a breaking point and I was getting near to mine.

In this first job I was not on watch but worked each day from eight in the morning to five at night. When the ship was in port, however, I always did the night watch from six o'clock at night to six in the morning.

The 2nd Engineer took me on one side, 'If you don't get some sleep in that time you are a b. fool but if you're caught you're a bigger one.'

I was in a quandary for one of my seniors was giving me contrary instructions. I did not relish the thought of sleeping in the daytime so I evolved a method of dozing in a standing position with my hand clutching a tool. The Chief Engineer noticed my apparent lack of sleep and his suspicions were aroused. He started to come down into the engine-room at different times through the night but he always found me at my tasks.

Always, that is, until I transferred to another ship, the S.S. Mohammedi. There came a time when his ship and Mohammedi were tied up side by side and late at night my former Chief looked over the rails and saw me asleep on deck. He shouted out and woke me up. I looked up in bewildered surprise to see him dancing up and down in a fury, giving vent to his frustration at not having been able to catch me on his own ship for I was able to cock a snook at him now.

My new ship was much bigger than the previous one and had the luxury of a lift between the engine-room and the upper deck. I devised a cunning method when on night watch of stopping the lift halfway and going to sleep. Whenever my Chief decided to carry out a nocturnal inspection the move-ment of the lift woke me up and when he came out of the lift he always found me busy at work. Despite this unauthorised slumber I still had to do with very little sleep at times. This has been good training for me, for life is so full nowadays that I begrudge hours spent in bed and gratefully find that I can manage with few hours sleep.

I was on the Mohammedi for about eighteen months. For half the year we took hajis, that is, pilgrims, to Jeddah and for the rest of the year were on charter. On the pilgrim trips we accommodated up to fifteen hundred hajis on temporary bunks in the hold. Many of them were elderly folk who had not been able to afford the voyage before but who were now so determined to make the pilgrimage before they died that they had sold their belongings in order to fulfil their dreams. Some of them were in no fit condition to travel and I suppose on average four or five died each time.

The ship was well prepared for such eventualities. We carried a supply of cast iron bars one of which was firmly strapped to the body which was then placed in a coffin with a bottom that swung open like a lid. This meant that the coffin itself could be lifted up from the water for further use in due course. We were supposed to stop the ship during the funeral but since this would have been a costly and time-consuming process we only went through the motions by briefly putting the engine telegraph astern and recording in the log that the engines were stopped.

Life on board, working with men of other races, presented me with a few cultural problems. One of these was my total abstention, as a Hindu, from alcoholic drinks. This was quite unacceptable to my fellow officers. I do not really understand why it is that drinkers are unhappy when teetotallers drink non-alcoholic beverages on social occasions but such, I regret, is often the case. I was not infrequently the victim of a disturbing amount of horseplay for my colleagues were determined to make me drink. One day four of them sat on me and tried to pour a half bottle of gin down my throat. But I spat it out. On another occasion they resorted to more deceptive methods. At a party I was handed an innocent-looking glass of coca-cola. Unbeknown to me, whisky had been mixed with it. I thought there was an unusual taste but my suspicions were not aroused. The result did not make me drunk but it gave me an unwonted Dutch courage which could have had disastrous consequences. With half a bottle of whisky in my stomach I loudly asserted to my tormentors that the reason I was an abstainer was not because I could not take alcohol. To prove my point I offered to bet a large sum of money that I could drink a whole bottle of whisky neat with no ill-effects. To the credit of the man to whom I made this absurd challenge, he would not let me proceed with such folly.

Once a deck officer was having his honeymoon on board. At nine-o'clock one night I met him and his wife in the passage on their way to their cabin.

'Hello,' I said cheerfully, 'Are you going to turn in?'

He glared at me whilst his young bride coloured up and averted her eyes. The next morning he gave me a severe dressing down for embarrassing his wife, but my remark had been made in all innocence and would not have been thought out of the way in India.

I was growing up fast. Underlying all my thoughts and feelings at this time was my ambition to get to the top of my profession. Within the depths of my being my ambition beat as powerfully and persistently as the rhythmic throb of the ship's engines. I continued to study hard and by the time I was twenty-four years old I had obtained Part A of my Chief Engineer's

Certificate. I had soon realised the important place that Lloyd's Register of Shipping held in the nautical world and I was determined to become an engineer surveyor working for them. When I confided my pipe-dream to my fellow engineers it was treated with facetious contempt.

'You? Working in London for Lloyds?' they cried incredulously. 'They would never take an Indian. Give up the idea straightaway. You'll never make it.'

Their disparaging remarks did not weaken my resolve one iota. If anything, they strengthened it. I knew that God had a plan for my life and I believed with all my heart that he was with me in this ambitious undertaking.

One of the ship's charter trips took us to London Docks. We arrived at Tilbury in March, 1953, on a day of thick fog. We could not see ten yards ahead; it was a real peasouper. To understand the traumatic effect that this weather had on me you would need to have lived in India. To me, it was unbelievable. How could English people possibly live in these conditions? Yet I still did not flinch from my determination to live in England. I was prepared to suffer.

'One day,' I vowed,' 'I will come back to England and get my Extra First-Class Certificate.'

Whilst in port one of the stewards, a Roman Catholic from Goa, asked permission to leave the ship to attend church. 'You converts are all the same,' grumbled the Captain. At this marked lack of enthusiasm the steward went below decks and reappeared with an encyclopaedia. From this book he showed the Captain that St Thomas brought Christianity to his part of the world at a time when the inhabitants of England were pagan. He was allowed to go to church!

On my return to India I found that my father had fallen ill and cancer of the cheek-bone had been diagnosed. He was taken to a hospital in Bombay where the growth was found to be in too advanced a condition for him to benefit from an operation. The family were anxious for everything possible to be done and in the end the doctors were persuaded to operate. But it was of no avail. He was taken back to Kerala to die and he himself knew that his time had come.

It was most unfortunate that it was in these distressing circumstances that I had to break the news to him which I knew would add to his anguish. I did not wish to do this but felt that time would admit no delay. So, taking the bull by the horns, I told him as gently as I could that my destiny lay in England. As I expected, he pleaded earnestly with me to remain in India with a local shipping firm and help support the family after his death. He was joined in these entreaties by the rest of the family. No one wanted me to go and they fought hard to keep me in India. But my mind was fully made up. Normally I would not have refused to obey my father's wishes and I was torn between loyalty to my family and my desire to do well in my profession. But I believed that God was leading me and it was after all my life that I had to live; so I made my last sad farewell.

The ironic situation, however, was that I did not have any money to travel to England. All the money I had earned at sea I had sent home to my father. So I prayed for help and the answer to my prayer came through Mr Anderson, now Works Manager. He got me a job on a lighthouse supply vessel, the S.S. Relume. I was flown to the Persian Gulf, boarded the ship as 2nd Engineer and travelled back to Bombay for a ship's refit which took three months. Then, after going back with the ship to the Gulf, I booked an air passage to London. This was to be a new beginning in my life.

6: In an alien land

Like a glittering diamond carpet the lights of London lay beneath me as the Argonaut from Bahrein began the descent to Heathrow. It was eleven o'clock at night on 1st May, 1956, and I had vindicated my self-promise to return. Of my future as a Lloyds engineer surveyor I had not the slightest doubt whatsoever, but what of the next few weeks, months, years? With just £104 in my pocket I had come to an alien land.

The coach deposited me at Victoria Air Terminal and I was alone. I had no job, no accommodation and it was now past midnight. I suffered a kind of loneliness I never wish to experience again. I had two slender props to my self-confidence. I had got on well with the captain of the lighthouse tender who was an ex-Naval commander and he had given me an excellent reference which should help me to obtain a post. Then a colleague had given me the address of the Missions to Seamen building where I was told I could try for accommodation as a mercantile marine officer. But beyond this, I had implicit trust in God; a trust, however, which was soon to be, if not exactly shaken, at least rocked a little.

I hurried to the Tube only to find to my great consternation that the Underground was closed for the night. The buses, too, had ceased running. I had with me forty-four pounds of luggage, my total worldly possessions, meagre enough in all conscience, but it was beginning to weigh a ton. What was I to do? I did not know a single soul and had no idea how to get from one place to the other. It was bad enough coming as a stranger into a city of a different culture but being abandoned on the pavement with not even one person around to ask the way made me feel as though I had landed on another planet. I became terribly frightened as I stood there in the darkness, cold and shivering in my summer suit. In desperation I prayed that all would come right.

I looked up and to my delight a taxi arrived from nowhere and stood right in front of me. I begged the driver to take me to the destination that was scribbled on a piece of paper. What a relief it was to find someone who knew the way. I did not find the taxi but the taxi found me. It was a miniature replica of the relief and peace I received when, years later, God found me.

Without thinking, I dismissed the taxi as soon as the address was reached and strode up to the door. But all was in darkness; everyone was in bed. Anxiously I knocked but no one came. My only hope, as it appeared to me, was for that door to swing open on its hinges so, heedless of the disturbance I was causing, I continued to beat a loud tattoo until after what seemed an eternity, the door was cautiously opened by a rather disgruntled and wary nightwatchman. He probably thought that he had a drunk on his hands and I could not blame him if he did. After hearing my story he stated emphatically that all the rooms were occupied and suggested that I try an establishment called the Flying Angel. I did not know where this was or how to get there so I clung like a leech to the idea of persuading the watchman to take pity on me. Eventually he came round to the point of view that the best way of getting a little peace was to take me in. He found an empty bed, after all, and I was soon asleep.

The next morning over breakfast some of my new companions kindly offered me useful advice on various shipping companies who might have vacancies. Top of the list, however, was not a shipping line but the Admiralty in Whitehall. So at ten o'clock I set out for the Director of Stores' office where personnel for the Royal Fleet Auxiliary vessels are engaged. I showed them my references and asked for an application form, intending to go back to the hostel to fill it out. I turned to go but to my surprise I was asked to fill out the form there and then. I was given an immediate interview and my testimonials created such a favourable impression that I was offered a post as 4th Engineer on a ship which was undergoing a refit on the Clyde. So within twenty-four hours of my arrival in a foreign land I had been offered both work and accommodation. God was very good to me.

Nevertheless, it was clear that he had no intention of molly-coddling me for when I arrived in Scotland I found that the ship's engines were turbine. Now up to then I had had no practical experience of turbines yet on me devolved responsibility for seeing that all the parts of the dismantled engines were correctly fitted. I studied the plans with great intensity and sweated blood lest I should make a mistake. Working from six in the morning to ten at night, I sometimes slept in my boiler suit and I toiled harder than I have ever done in my life.

After the refit we sailed to Curacao and transported oil to places like Baltimore, Boston and Jersey City. When the 2nd Engineer fell ill I was promoted to take his place over the head of the 3rd Engineer who, not unnaturally, was distinctly unhappy about the situation. This did not make for easy relationships but most of the officers were friendly to me. The crew were fellow countrymen and this was a great help. For about three and a half years I worked for the Royal Fleet Auxiliary serving in four ships altogether. I lived frugally and did not take any leave during the whole of this period. I sent money home to India and so confident was I of ending up at Lloyds Register that I opened a bank account with the branch of Lloyds Bank that was situated next door!

My boyhood ambition to travel was now being fulfilled in good measure. We sailed to many parts of the world including North and South America, the Mediterranean, African coast and the Far East. Yet it was not travel in any real sense. In port I often only went ashore to do odd shopping and in any event a ship's officer has little opportunity to explore in depth.

Sometimes, to amuse myself, I would join with some of the crew in fishing. I remember how in Botany Bay the Chinese cook and I dropped overboard a baited hook attached to a nylon cord: a very simple type of fishing but it brought results. Soon we were hauling up a shark-sized fish, the kind that sea-anglers are photographed with. Sure enough, someone duly produced a camera and I still have that photo in my possession today. That night we held a feast at which this fish was the guest of honour! It tasted delicious and there was enough for the entire ship's company.

Life on board ship was for me a paradox. There was both luxury and hard, unpleasant work. It was wonderful to get up and at the press of a button have coffee, made carefully to my liking, brought to me by the steward; the bath run to the right temperature; shoes polished till they shone. Food was always served as in a five star hotel. There was no commuting to work in a crowded train or through traffic jams. After work I had lots of time to myself – no gardening, decorating or household repairs to be done.

One week I was in England and the next week in the sunny tropics. I was always on the move meeting people of different cultures and life styles. Earth became a global city.

Sitting on the deck all alone at night after watch was often a memorable experience. A moon-lit sky above, its reflection dancing on gently ruffled waters as the ship moved slowly in the stillness of the night; the sweet sound of the engine whispering like soft music; the rhythmic beat of the waves on the stern of the ship; the innumerable stars slowly rocking in time to the ship's gentle pitch; these are treasured memories. I could but drink to the brim of the beauty of God's creation, bow my head in awe at the expanse of the universe and marvel at the wisdom of the Creator's hand behind it all.

Often on a clear night I wondered where space ended and when it had all begun. Not having read the Bible I longed to find out how God created the world, when it would come to an end and what would happen to us eventually.

An unforgettable memory that I cherish is of standing at the stern as the ship left the harbour, watching the hustle and bustle disappear from sight as the ship sailed away into new horizons. Often, as I enjoyed those precious moments, I wondered whether death was as peaceful as this, simply a moving away from the materialistic world, from what one once thought important and clung to so selfishly without a thought of its transience. It gave me a sense of proportion to realise that earthly life is only a journey from birth to death and there is more to life than a few years of existence. We are indeed in an alien land when we look at life in the light of Eternity. As a Hindu I was afraid to die because I knew that I had to face God and answer him for all my thoughts, words and deeds; judgement is very real to a Hindu.

Just as the contemplation of natural beauty brought disturbing thoughts so life at sea had its ups and downs. When the sea was rough the ship rolled so badly that it frequently appeared to be at the point of capsizing. It was a terrifying experience.

We had instructions to change the exhaust valves on the main engine after a thousand hours running. We would stop the engine exactly after that period irrespective of where we were; it might be in the Red Sea with a temperature of 128° F. in the shade. It was then real murder; you could fry an egg on top of the engine. Everybody turned to work, doing fifteen minutes in the engine room and then going up to stand under the hosepipe to cool off for twenty minutes. We could have done the job more quickly and more efficiently in port but that was not to be. Later on I remembered this, and it taught me a lesson. Religious people who work by the letter of the law, as the Pharisees did in the time of Jesus, and not by the spirit of it, can do great harm to the cause of true religion.

Once, between New Zealand and Singapore, we had a major breakdown. A piston broke off and smashed the cylinder top and we had to isolate that cylinder in rough weather. It took us three days and we worked round the clock with only a couple of hours sleep in between.

Loneliness was our chief enemy. To my fellow officers, married with a family, it must have been unbearable. Perhaps that is why men at sea are prone to take to drink. Whisky and gin could be bought duty free, and were thirty pence a bottle in those days. It was not necessary to pay cash but only to sign a chit, the money being deducted from the salary at the end of each voyage.

Once at Singapore a visiting commander from a Naval ship remarked to our Chief Enginer, 'I see your Second doesn't touch a drop.'

Quick came the reply from the Chief, 'If he starts drinking, I have to stop!'

Well, someone always stayed sober on board and seldom anyone got really drunk.

This city brings me unhappy memories. I was a young man, as yet unmarried, living an unnatural life in exclusively masculine company. Up to then I had lived a pure and ascetic existence in accordance with the best tenets of Hinduism but one night desire welled strong within me. I went ashore, made my way to the red light district of the city and entered a brothel. Madame lined up several of her girls for me to make my choice but then somewhat to my astonishment and certainly to theirs, I turned round and walked out into the street. To this day I do not really know why I did. Was it loss of nerve at the last moment? Or was it my religious inhibitions asserting themselves? Or was it, as I like to think, the hand of God gently guiding me? All I know is that I am very glad that I did what I did, though I was sorely tempted to remain.

Prostitution is the bane of the mercantile marine. At ship parties in Sydney, Wellington and elsewhere girls would come on board and try to seduce the officers. Always I resisted their blandishments successfully although there were times when I was strongly tempted to give way. I recall one day in the Seychelles when a sister of one of the crew came on board and I was asked to 'show her the ship' which is a euphemism for 'go to bed with her'! She was quite attractive and I managed to palm her off on the Chief Engineer who was only too willing because he had an old hag whom he passed off in turn to the 'sparks'! All very sordid but this was how life was lived at times.

We were once at Wellington in New Zealand, berthed right near a residential area. On a number of nights I stood on deck looking at those beautifully-lit homes and thinking how lucky those men were to have a home to go to in the evening and a family of their own to love them. These lights made me dream wistfully of the home that might be mine one day.

Later, whilst I was on the long night watches tending the engines, my mind more and more frequently turned to thoughts of settling down to mar-

ried life. From my college days I was madly infatu-
ated with the daughter of my cousin who was in
Burma. When I left Kerala for good she was in her
early teens and I was fascinated by her natural charm
and beauty. Her parents, too, were wonderful people
and I knew that she had inherited their nature. The
more I pondered and dreamed, the more did my
thoughts focus, almost to the point of obsession, on
Susheila. Yes, she was the wife for me.

The next step now, the only step, was to obtain her
parents' permission. I was sufficiently Westernised
by this time to make my own request and not follow
the traditional Indian fashion of waiting for my
parents to arrange a marriage for me. Whilst I was at
Bombay I had corresponded with her parents and
now I wrote to them again. Great was my joy to learn
that they would give their blessing to my proposal.
Perhaps their daughter herself was happy to accept
whatever her parents thought best for her and from
that time onwards the two of us wrote to each other
regularly. When the ship returned to Britain I
bought a five diamond engagement ring and sent it
out to her to seal the engagement.

It only remained for a wedding date to be fixed but
because of the uncertainty of my voyages some time
necessarily elapsed before this could be arranged. At
last, the opportunity came when the ship I was on
received orders to proceed to Bombay for boiler
cleaning. I sent a cable to my wife-to-be's parents and
the whole family travelled to the port for the wedding. My ship sailed into Bombay Harbour on 21st
May, 1959, and three days later we were married.
The exact time of a Hindu wedding is fixed after
consultation with astrologers who chose the auspi-

cious time called 'Muhurtham'. According to the astrologer there was only one day during my stay in Bombay that we could possibly have got married. Indeed, even for the marriage to take place, the horoscopes of my wife and myself had to agree.

A wedding ceremony varies from State to State but usually consists of two parts the first of which is held in the temple and the second in the family home. The temple ritual, when the marriage is symbolically centred upon God, is elaborate and beautiful. The ceremony in the home has many simple, symbolic acts to celebrate the marriage union. It concludes with the piling up of wedding presents, and with feasting.

On the night after my wedding a hall was hired for a big reception. I had to sail the following day to New Zealand while my wife remained in India. Meanwhile, later in the year, my ship was sold to a Hong Kong shipping line and a passage back to England was arranged for me on the P. & O. ship S.S. Carthage. I saw the opportunity for my wife to join me at Bombay and accordingly I booked a passage for her. So our belated honeymoon, if you can call it that, was spent seven months late on board ship. The sea was rough, the circumstances disturbingly strange for Susheila and there was almost no privacy.

We arrived in London on a bitterly cold December day and the ensuing months were to prove a traumatic experience for my young bride in more ways than one. She found the climate almost unendurable. I could not stand the cold either but I at least did have other matters on which to concentrate my mind. The first of my teenage ambitions had now been realised, I had married a beautiful girl. The second aim, to be a Lloyds surveyor, was, I felt, well on the way to realisation. The third goal, to know God, would have to wait a while.

Whilst serving with the Royal Fleet Auxiliary I had not been idle. The Chief Engineer's Certificate for both steam and diesel engines was safely in my pocket but I wanted the Extra Chief Engineer's Certificate. I had already notified Lloyds that as soon as I had obtained the Extra Certificate, which I confidently informed them would be in 1961, I should be available to join their staff. I chose to study in South Shields, not the warmest of places to spend a British winter, because my younger brother Suku who had come to England three years earlier, was serving an apprenticeship at South Shields. He was living as paying guest with a lady named Mrs Curley, the widow of a Royal Navy Captain who had died at sea. She had kindly agreed to provide accommodation for us as well. It so happened that when we arrived in London she was staying with relatives at Upminster so we joined her there, together with my brother who had come down to meet us, and we all travelled North together. The streets of South Shields were covered with snow and the empty house was bitterly cold. My wife went into our room and cried her eyes out.

Three facts above all others astonished me about England. One was the coldness of the climate, another was the hard work done by English women. In India we were used to seeing the memsahibs walking around with their noses in the air, waited on by a team of servants. Here in England servants were almost non-existent and the wives of high-ranking men were not ashamed to work. The third fact was the generally high standard of honesty.

In South Shields I had six months' paid leave, the money from which had to last the two of us for eighteen months! Our housekeeping of necessity had to be frugal in the extreme. I spent long hours in study, deciding to go for a Part A in January 1961 and Part B in July of that year. The lecturers said that I would not be able to do it; nobody had for the last seven years. I studied each day at the College from eight-thirty in the morning to nine-thirty at night, then went home to supper after which there was always more study until nearly two o'clock in the morning. It was far from a pleasant existence for a young wife in an alien culture without friends and with a husband who only lived for study.

Before long Mrs Curley was unfortunately taken ill and went into hospital. She was a wonderful Christian woman who never tried to push her religion down our throats but who, I found out long afterwards, had been praying secretly for us daily. She had a friend, Jim Kyle, who was a lay preacher and leader of a Bible study group and she asked him and his wife to join her in prayer for us. When, five years later, Jim read of my conversion in a Christian newspaper he could hardly believe for joy. He put a long distance phone call through to Lloyds to ask me personally if it was really me that the article referred to and to express his delight that their prayers had been so wonderfully answered.

Sadly, Mrs Curley's condition deteriorated, and it was not long before she died. We were upset by her death, and missed her sorely. I sat for my exam and then my money ran out. But I found a temporary job whilst waiting for the exam results.

Then at last, I learnt that I had obtained the coveted Extra Certificate getting only five marks less than the winner of the gold medal and cash award. The way was clear to renew my application to Lloyds which I did with satisfactory results. On 12th December, 1961 I walked proudly up the stone steps of the imposing entrance to the building which housed Lloyds Register of Shipping in the City of London. In the spacious entrance hall I glanced with admiration at the massive pillars of brown marble as I waited to be conducted along the corridors to my office. All the long hours spent in burning the midnight oil, all the monotony of months passed in the hard grind of study, all the patient years of waiting, lay in the past. The 'impossible' dreams of my youth had come to fruition at last. I had arrived!

7: Right about face

Meanwhile, my spiritual pilgrimage continued, though at this stage much of it was not at the conscious level. On the surface there was no indication at all that one day in the not far distant future I would make a dramatic and life-changing switch from the faith of my forbears to the religion which in my understanding then was a Western one. But I believe that God through the Holy Spirit was even then at work in my subconscious, directing my deep desire to find the truth and harnessing my powerful ambitions to worthier ends.

But, become a Christian? The very thought would have been anathema to me. Perhaps the principal obstacle to such a transformation was the fact that what little I knew of Christianity was a garbled tangle of misunderstandings.

A police patrol car stopped a motorist one night and the officer came to him and asked, 'How long have you been driving without a rear light, sir?'

The driver got out of the car, went back and looked. 'Oh no,' he groaned and tore his hair in despair.

Puzzled at this extreme reaction the policeman tried to reassure him. 'Come now, sir,' he said sympathetically, 'there's no need to take it so badly, it's important but it isn't that serious.'

'Oh, isn't it?' retorted the motorist. 'Then pray tell me what's happened to my caravan!'

The policeman and the driver misunderstood each other. Now I have found that Christianity is one of the most misunderstood subjects today. For myself, I do not think that people can be blamed for not understanding Christianity. If you had come to me a few years ago and predicted that I would become a Christian I would have been frightened to death. I would have begged God to protect me from the Christian fanatics. Such was my ignorance of Jesus Christ.

I had as much knowledge of the Bible as I suspect many of you have of the Hindu sacred writings – none at all. A little matter like that did not stop me from rejecting Christianity out of hand nor from avidly accepting the criticisms of others who had not read it either. Of course, I had heard that Jesus Christ was crucified and I even felt sorry for the poor bloke hanging there. But I thought that Jesus died only for Christians; I did not know that he gave his life for all who turn to him.

I was misled by the weak witness of many nominal Christians in my part of India. They did not seem to me to take their devotions very seriously. Easter, it appeared to me, was a time for them to indulge in drinks when the risen Christ was forgotten amongst the parties and celebrations. On Good Friday Christians went around in mourning; they wore black ties and armbands and looked miserable. Even the name for Good Friday is *Duka Valli* meaning Sad Friday. They never exhibited victory and joy in their daily living. Religion for them appeared to be a burden and a chain on their ankle.

Moreover, compared with the ascetic restraint of many Hindus, some of the Christians I knew were leading lives of sensual indulgence and the business men, instead of loving each other, were at each other's throats. I looked at Christians and I thought to myself, if that is Christianity I do not want it. If I had read a Gospel and looked at Jesus instead it would have been a different story altogether.

Even as a young boy I was full of resentment against missionaries. Why do they come and bother us, I thought, we don't ask them to become Hindus. Do you know I used to be so perplexed by this that I would sit down and try to puzzle it out. I concluded that missionaries were earning their salvation; every time they won another convert I thought that a mark was chalked up in Heaven for them.

This, then, was my spiritual state when I entered the church of St Helens on a spring day in 1965. The address given by the Rev Dick Lucas was a revelation to me. I heard for the first time that Jesus died for the Hindus, he died for the Moslems, he died for the Buddhists, he died for everybody, he even died for *me*, so that I might live after death with him.

Dick went on to say that God had done everything necessary for anyone to find God today and know him personally. It is not what I can do for God that is important but what God has done for me. I knew that Jesus had died but I did not know why he had died, I did not know that had he died for me. If I had died on that Tuesday night as a Hindu, I knew that I would not stand a chance of getting to Heaven. But according to the word of God I could be assured of a place there if I turned to Jesus.

So in the course of a fairly short address I had

learnt two facts which to me were absolutely astonishing. First, that Jesus had given his life for me, personally, in order that I might have eternal life; secondly I learnt that I could not earn salvation because it was free. The effect on me was instantaneous and staggering. The Holy Spirit bore witness in my heart that the word of God read aloud by the preacher was true.

As I sat on my chair I turned my thoughts to Jesus and said, 'I'll have a try, Lord, I'll have a try. I don't know how to pray, but you help me and I'll try. I want to obey you. Please help me to belong to you.'

And help me he did. Not only then but ever since in all sorts of ways. When I returned to the office I got into conversation about spiritual matters with one of my colleagues. During the talk I understood that he and the head of our department went to the lunch hour talks at St Helens. I asked John whether it was possible for me to join them and craftily failed to inform him that I had already been.

We duly went and from that time onwards I never missed going on Tuesdays. These lunchtime meetings were a great joy to me.

John said, 'To think that I had been sitting here for a year and a half praying for you, hoping that somehow we could go to St Helens together but I didn't have the guts to ask.'

Perhaps he was wrong not to have asked me. Perhaps we do tend to pray and leave it at that, when God is requiring some practical action from us. On the other hand, there is a right time and a wrong time and I do not think that John need have reproached himself. I do not honestly think he could have successfully persuaded me before then.

There was at that time another series of lectures on Thursdays given by Dick Lucas' associate, David MacInnes. God really spoke to me when David expounded from chapter two of Galatians. I saw that God was instructing me that I was enslaved unnecessarily by a weight of legalism. He was telling me that although I could not win my own way to Heaven by obeying the law I need not worry because in Christ he had done it all.

One day shortly after that I said to my business colleague, 'You know, John, I would like to read a Bible.'

He did not waste any time in making a present of a Bible. As he handed it to me I noticed a piece of material sticking out. 'I have put a bookmark in John's Gospel, Vijay,' he said. 'I want you to start reading from there.'

I am mighty glad that he gave me this advice, otherwise I would have started from Genesis and got bogged down in Leviticus and Numbers. The day following our visit to St Helens, John took me to a meeting of Lloyds own Christian Union. It was a Bible study and discussion group. There were about twenty people there including one man who apparently made a habit of asking disturbing, difficult questions.

True to form, during the discussion this man asked, 'Why is that some people who have become Christian and are going on very well in the Christian life, lose their faith and reject Christianity?'

I can vividly remember the reaction of the other nineteen. They turned round and stared at him with disapproving frowns and loud 'shhhs!' One of them articulated their feelings when he said sharply,

'We've got a newcomer here, don't ask such stupid questions.'

Well, it did not worry me. As a matter of fact, it intrigued me and I wanted to find out the answer to that question. So I began to pray earnestly to God, 'God show me, if I come to you and I belong to you, is it possible for me to reject you?'

I wanted to find a real answer and do you know, as I prayed a wonderful thing happened. I had a kind of vision. It was most definitely not a dream for I was wide awake. I saw three people walking along and ahead of them but to the side, was a door. One of them was clearly not interested in the door for he was walking aimlessly around. The second man was walking towards the door which the third person had already passed through.

I heard a little voice which said, 'You know, Vijay, the person who is walking around is the person who is not interested in God or Christianity. The person who is walking towards the door is a person who is seeking God, who is interested in spiritual matters, who may look like a Christian and may even be going to church and saying his prayers but he is not a Christian. The one who has crossed through the door is a Christian who has put himself in God's hands. Once someone has gone through the door he cannot turn back and you, Vijay, have passed through the door.'

I was terribly excited about this and as soon as I next saw John I told him about my vision. He looked the surprise he felt. 'You know, Vijay, that's funny. Jesus himself said, "I am the door".'

I had not even read the Bible to know that Jesus said that. A rather strange start but that was the beginning of my life with my Lord. The vision was a confirmation of my experience in St Helens. This incident will have shown you that I had not been swept into Christianity on a wave of emotionalism. I certainly possess strong emotions but that is very different from emotionalism. I am also a thinking man and I like to have a reason for my faith. So my transition from Hinduism to Christianity was not effected without deep inward questioning, and doubts and problems arose from time to time. I dealt with these thoughtfully and prayerfully one at a time.

When I came to the end of St John's Gospel I was thrilled to find that after Jesus Christ was crucified he rose from the dead and is alive today. I thought that if Jesus Christ is alive today then we have got absolute proof that there is life after death. But then doubts arose in my mind.

It started with niggling little questions. 'Vijay, how do you really know?'

Well, I thought, I know for certain that he lived because it is 1965 years after his birth. The calendar testifies to his life. History bears witness to his existence.

'But how can you be sure that he's alive today?'

I had not been brought up to the Bible. I felt that I could have trusted the Hindu scriptures which my parents taught me but as yet the Bible was not as deeply ingrained in my life as the Hindu writings. How could I honestly say that I knew Jesus was alive? How, indeed, could I be sure? Truth is paramount, so for a period of weeks I diligently and prayerfully sought the truth.

'Jesus, show me please if you are alive.'

About three months later I was trying to get a climbing rose for my back garden. We have a semi-detached house, you see, and our garage, which is at the back, has a brick wall which can be seen from the kitchen. So I suggested to my wife that it would be a good idea to get some English roses to cover the garage wall. Then when we get visitors, friends coming in and hopefully helping wash up in the kitchen, they will gaze out of the window and say, 'Look, lovely English roses.'

I was sitting in my front room on the sofa turning the pages of a nursery catalogue to find out what roses I could buy. There were Yellow Speck, Golden Ranger and many others but what really caught my eye, right in the centre page, was Ena Harkness, a beautiful crimson rose, huge, as big as an outstretched hand, and the catalogue notes said it is one of the most fragrant roses among the climbers.

As I looked at this rose a little voice said, 'Vijay, if God can create a beautiful flower from a seed which has neither beauty nor perfume, it is not difficult for God to bring Jesus back to life.'

I thought then that I see the miracles of God and take them for granted. I believe them; I do not ask questions. If I were to bring together all the scientists of the world and give them all the equipment that they want they would not be able to produce a seed from ammonia, phosphate, calcium and nitrogen which can result in a flower, but God does it.

Then I thought of my elder son who was eighteen months old at that time. Suppose I were to bring him up in a big concrete building away from nature and feed him on tinned and frozen foods. Suppose, in consequence, he does not see any vegetation at all.

Then, when he is sixteen years of age I take a flower and its seed to him and say, 'Look, son, God can create this flower from this seed.' If I did this he would not believe it because he had not seen it. Yet it would be true.

When I opened my catalogue I was not looking for an answer from God to my questioning but to my surprised delight he provided one when I was not expecting it and the answer was in a rose. I thought, it is just as though I had lost a key and suddenly I opened a drawer and there was the key.

I looked at the television in the corner of the room and I thought that most of us have no idea how television works. We just switch on the set and see what is happening in Australia and in America, and we believe what we see.

Then I thought that if I could have evaporated myself as in Doctor Who, gone back two thousand years and walked with Jesus and the disciples, I would not have found them asking Jesus how he accomplished the miracles.

Peter never came and asked Jesus, 'Come on, Jesus, how did you give sight to that blind man who never saw in his life?'

John never came and said, 'How did you make the lame man, who never walked in his life, jump up and down with joy.'

No, they believed as they saw. It did happen and we do not have to see in order to believe.

I remember that I was so excited by these thoughts that I ran out of my house and looked next door to where my neighbour was mowing the lawn and I went up to him and said, 'Ian, do you know what an elephant is?'

He looked at me quite surprised.

'If I say you can count a hundred elephants and put them on a seed as big as an orange pip would you believe it?' I asked

It was quite clear that he thought I was mad. Can you imagine someone coming to you and asking a stupid question like that? But I was too excited by my discovery to care what he thought.

I ran back to my bedroom and took my elephant seed which I had brought from India. This is a hollow seed the size of an orange pip, with a little ivory. I took this seed out to him.

'Look here,' I said, 'There are a hundred elephants carved in ivory inside this minute seed. Now just as you can plainly see that these elephants are there so Jesus was real to the disciples – they saw him, touched him, had breakfast with him. The really important thing is that Jesus Christ is alive today.'

You know, my poor neighbour looked absolutely bewildered. He said, 'Vijay, what are you talking about?'

So I had to begin at the beginning and explain to him what had just happened in my front room.

Then I said, 'Ian, if you go to your neighbour, John, and tell him that Vijay showed you a hundred elephants carved from ivory in a small seed you will have a lot of convincing to do. He won't believe you but despite this it will still be true.'

During a casual conversation in my office a colleague remarked, 'Vijay, I wish I had your blind faith.'

Immediately I corrected him that my faith is not blind. It's based on the historical facts of the birth, crucifixion and resurrection of Jesus Christ and on the certainty of God's promises.

It was in ways like this that I wrestled with my doubts about my new faith and with God's help won through to a glorious certainty. I soon had a desire to be baptised and this was arranged for 27 July, 1965. I had what I now know to be a naive belief that all English people were Christians. I was so pleased at the thought of my forthcoming baptism that I informed many of my English friends and invited them to come. Well, they just laughed at me.

One of them said, 'Vijay, don't get so excited, this is only a phase. You will get over it soon. Come and see me in six months' time.'

'No, no, that's not the case at all,' I replied, 'it's real.'

'Look here,' he said, 'I'm an Anglican brought up in a public school and I was a member of the school choir but the only spirit-filled life I enjoyed in the Anglican church was the communion wine which I drank when no one was looking.'

That was typical of the reaction of my friends. They thought that enthusiasm ought not to be associated with Christianity. To many churchgoers religion is dull, lifeless and boring but strangely enough they seem to prefer it that way, believing that to be enthusiastic about one's religious convictions is not in the best of taste. The greatest condemnation that the Anglican hierarchy could make of John Wesley in the eighteenth century was that he was enthusiastic. For myself, I am a man who does not believe in bottling up emotion. God gave us feelings as well as the powers of thought and will, and so I firmly believe that it is entirely right to be enthusiastic about the deep truths of Christianity. Even the origin of the word, *en theos*, full of God, justifies it.

My Hindu friends also strongly disapproved of my decision, but that, I suppose, was only to be expected.

I remember one of them coming to me and after I had been telling him that Jesus is alive. He said, 'Come on, Vijay, you are an engineer surveyor – you are a man who has to reason out things by way of your profession – you of all people can't tell me that Christians can gain salvation by believing a theory that Jesus died for you or accepting a doctrine that Jesus Christ is your Lord and Saviour. Come, come, you should know better than that.'

You may be surprised to learn that I could not answer him. But, remember, I was only very young in the faith and had only just crossed the tremendous gulf which separates the two religions. My policy for a long time has been that if I am out of my depth I keep my mouth shut lest I drown. So I changed the subject quickly.

'Very nice weather we are having now, don't you think, that is, for England,' I added quickly.

Then I went home and in my usual way I began to pray, 'Please God, show me, is it a theory or a doctrine?' I began to read John's Gospel again and by the time that I had come to the fifteenth chapter I found that salvation for Christians is not a theory or a formula but a sound truth based on a precious promise of God.

Again and again he promises that when we come to him, he will look after us. We can see this happening in the Bible. Take Peter and John, for example. The fourth chapter of Acts tells us that when the crowd saw the boldness of Peter and John and perceived that they were uneducated, common men, they recognised that they had been with Jesus. Something happened to them, it changed their lives and that is what happened to me.

Jesus came into my life; he touched every part of it; he turned it upside down. For thirty-five years I had tried to lead a good Hindu life – I did not smoke, I did not drink and I prayed to God every day. When I got up in the morning I would ask God to help me, before I fell asleep at night I would say a short prayer and in major decisions I always sought his guidance. Yet I never knew him until Jesus found me. I had an excellent job in the City, a house in suburbia, wife, sons, enough money in the bank to meet my needs but, although I was not the worrying type, I never enjoyed life until Jesus found me.

Jesus said, 'I have come that they might have life and that they might have it more abundantly.' I have proved those words to be gloriously true.

8: On course

You will have gathered that my growth as a Christian was a gradual, at times almost imperceptible, process. It was, I believe, none the worse for that. Slowly but surely my Christian faith was being built up on sound foundations. The story of the sower scattering seed is relevant here. There had to be time for the seed to germinate; time for the temporary seed-leaves to grow before the permanent leaves could form; time for the delicate young roots to toughen as well as lengthen. A too rapid growth above ground might well have meant that the roots would have been inadequate to sustain the plant. No, I do not regret the slow growth on the surface for I know now that deep within me the roots were growing strong.

Changing the metaphor completely, I was conscious that the vessel of my life had changed direction and I had an inner assurance that I was now on course for the distant harbour that all along had been the haven of my desire. But obstacles were still in the way. Fierce currents, shoals, reefs and submerged rocks littered the route ahead but somehow I knew that if I trusted him, the Pilot I had taken on board would see me safely through.

I certainly did not find the Christian way of life a walkover. Have you noticed that when God calls you along a certain direction it is not long before opposition of all kinds comes your way. It is the age-old battle of good and evil. Even Paul found it to be so and expressed his experience in unforgettable words when he said, 'When I would do good, evil is present with me.' Who was I, to think that I should be able to avoid this battle? In the last chapter I mentioned one of two instances of the ridicule I received and the doubts which assailed my mind. That state of affairs continued.

In times of difficulty I always turned to the Bible for help. On reflection it was of great assistance that the Bible was an unknown book to me. I came to it fresh, without any preconceived ideas or prejudices, and the words came alive. One day I was eagerly explaining to a Hindu friend how God speaks personally through the Bible and how it is so applicable to today's needs.

A slow smile spread across his face and he said, 'Vijay, you are a man who has passed the extra first class engineer's exam, how can you believe the Adam and Eve story, for example? You don't take it seriously, do you? Science, evolution, the work of Darwin, all disprove the Bible.'

At that time I knew very little indeed about the Bible. So I asked God to show me how to explain the Adam and Eve story to my friend. God chose to answer me in a very practical way through my work. It so happened that it was at this time that the liner Queen Elizabeth II was on the drawing boards. Now my job is to approve the designs of ship's engines, boilers and crankshafts. On my desk on that day was one of the plans of the boiler of the Q.E.II although I knew it only as John Brown 732 because it had not yet been named. I knew that this was one of the largest passenger liners being built for Cunard and as I looked at the plans I said to myself in surprise, 'This ship is so big!'

As I was checking part of the boiler a little voice said, 'Do you know, Vijay, if you had to write a book on the construction of this ship it would be twenty or thirty volumes. This is the biggest you have approved.'

This was perfectly true. Take the funnel, for example. Very many formulae have been worked out to get it right. For example, one funnel sits inside another. If you were to walk on the deck of the Q.E.II in your dinner jacket or evening dress you could be sure that the soot from the funnel would not fall on you. The turbulence of the wind is worked out in such a way that the wind takes the soot away and drops it a mile from the ship. A description of the curtains in all their variety would take another book. The upholstery would be another two books. Engine rooms would be a few books. A problem with the engine, which the Q.E.II had after the launching, would require another book.

When we turn to the account of the creation of the world in Genesis we find it written on two pages. The Bible is not a scientific book giving us the origin of all things – it is a religious book bringing us to God. If I want to explain to my son what an atom is I need six pictures. Can you imagine what would happen if God wrote a book on how he created the world? I will tell you. We would never get to him. Such information could not be contained in a book. Genesis speaks about God creating the world and this most definitely is not contrary to science whatever some pseudo scientists may say. So in this way God made clear to me the fallacious reasoning of my Hindu friend.

One of the biggest trials that can come to a Christian young in the faith is that of a serious illness. He has been told that God is a loving father. Instinctively he knows that ill health is not part of God's plan for mankind; it represents malfunctioning somewhere along the line in parts which were originally created perfect by the divine Engineer. The patient wonders why he should be picked out as the victim just when a rich, full life is opening up to him. Where does illness come from? Why does God allow it? How is it that the intercessory prayers of the patient's friends often do not seem to make any noticeable difference? These are some of the questions that buzz around in the mind of the bewildered new-found Christian like a swarm of angry bees. My experience, however, was rather different.

It was in December, 1965, only about six months after I had been baptised, that I began to get a terrible, searing pain under my ribs. My family doctor did not waste any time in sending me to the hospital for tests. Fifty x-rays were taken without revealing anything significant. Then on the 7th March, 1966, a re-examination of one of the plates showed a shadow near the spine. I was admitted to hospital the next day without even time to go to my office in the City to say goodbye to my colleagues.

The doctors said it could be cancer. Cancer! The very name was like the muffled tolling of a funeral bell. My father had died in 1955 of cancer and I had wept. My mother had died in 1961 of cancer and I broke my heart. My grandfather died of cancer – my whole family was cancer-ridden. And now me. I know that if I had remained a Hindu I should have been panic-stricken. I was convinced in my own mind that I had about two years to live because both my parents died two years after the disease had been detected. Yet such was the tremendous strength I received from Jesus that I did not even bat an eyelid. I thanked God from the bottom of my heart that Jesus found me before I entered the hospital.

The surgeon operated early in April. It was discovered that my spine was affected so I had to lie prostrate on a board bed for twenty weeks. Do you know those were the best twenty weeks of my life? God gave me this long period to rest quietly and read his Word. There were no decisions to make, no trains to catch, no visiting to do, no washing up, no decorating, no gardening – just endless time to soak up the Scriptures. Through them God began to speak to me, it was terrific. When we read the Bible asking for God's help it comes to us and brings happiness. That, anyway, was my experience.

Mind you, I had pain of course – at times it was terrible pain. The injections were extremely painful but I could bear them. I thought about the cross, about Jesus dying for me. I saw the soldiers placing the crown of thorns on his head; brutal hands pressing it down so that the sharp points pierced and lacerated his brow; drops of blood emerging and slowly trickling down his face. I saw them buffeting him with their fists and mocking him. Then I gathered with the crowd at the hill called Calvary and watched with anguish as nails were hammered into his palms. I listened with awe and wonder as I heard him begging forgiveness for his persecutors and torturers and I knew that he bore all this agony for me.

After that, the needle was a pin prick by comparison. I remember the ward sister saying, 'Vijay, you're the only one who doesn't complain.' She did not know my secret.

The weeks went by and still I remained flat on my back. They made a special stand for me so that with the aid of a periscopic lens I could not only read the Bible but could also turn the pages. I was able to read the Bible right through.

One day in the x-ray department the technician who was adjusting the instrument asked me, 'Vijay, how long have you been here now?'

'Oh, about seventeen weeks,' I replied.

'You must be bored stiff, musn't you?'

'No, no, it's exciting,' I responded eagerly. 'I'm reading the Bible. Have you read the Bible? Do you know Jesus?'

She stared at me blankly. The expression on her face plainly showed that she had serious doubts about my sanity.

She walked over to the other nurse and said, 'You know that bloke Vijay over there. What do you think he's just asked me? He wanted to know if I read the Bible and whether I know Jesus. He's nuts!'

But the Bible is exciting, isn't it? My wife, of course, noticed my happiness and said, 'You're enjoying life, aren't you? When are you coming back?'

I think perhaps that she was a little envious. You see, she was still a Hindu at that time and in addition her circumstances were rather difficult. She had to manage the house on her own, look after our eighteen month old son, do the work of two people and then come and visit me.

She was not the only person to observe my enjoyment. My colleague who had said that my christian faith would not last six months, came to visit me.

He said, 'Vijay, you seem quite happy, you must be very much better. When are you coming back to work?'

I looked him in the face and replied triumphantly, 'Do you remember, my friend, that you said my faith wouldn't last six months? Well, you were wrong. And not only that, my faith is strong enough even to give me joy through all this time of weariness and pain.'

I was not a mature Christian who knew everything about the Bible; I was not a churchwarden or anything like that. In many ways I had not much of a clue. All I did was put my hand in the Lord's and let him carry me through. What a joy that was. I knew that Jesus was real when he came into my life and remained with me through all the problems and difficulties. He not only stayed with me but strengthened me.

I do not, however, want to give the impression that it was not a testing time. Of course I had questions and doubts. I remember asking God, 'Lord, what about my wife if I am going to die in two years' time?'

The doctors told her that if they had to give me radium treatment they would have to transfer me from the local hospital to one in London where there were facilities for this treatment. This brought back my fears that I had not very much longer to live.

I renewed my pleas to the Lord and back the answer came, 'Well, Vijay, you weren't born with a silver spoon in your mouth but look at where you are now, a senior engineer surveyor with Lloyds. If I could look after you up to now and if I want to take you away from this world, I know how to look after your wife and family. I have only loaned them to you for a limited number of years but they are mine for all eternity.'

It was a marvellous feeling to realise that although I was in hospital in a foreign land with a young wife and son dependent on me, God would look after us. I had confidence that if God wanted me with him then he would know how to compensate my family and give them more joy in spite of my absence. I could trust them in his hands. I recall reading in Philippians, 'For me to live is Christ and to die is gain.' Those were my thoughts also.

Because many people were praying for my Hindu wife she had the strength to go through all the problems and the ordeal. When I recovered and returned home I realised that God was at work in my family life. But I had come to understand that he was not going to use me, at least not in a direct way. This was forcibly brought home to me by a small incident which, though amusing in retrospect, was rather terrifying at the time.

It happened before I went to the hospital. My wife wanted to learn to drive a car and I decided to teach her. I sat in the passenger seat beside her and we began with a few runs around the estate roads while she familiarised herself with the steering. When she had got used to this we went out on to the main road. After some distance the road narrows and as we approached I noticed a very large lorry parked outside a parade of shops.

I turned to my wife, 'Now, Susheila, would you slow down.'

'What do we want to slow down for?' she asked me

in a leisurely manner, not attempting to respond.

'Will you stop?' I replied with a note of increased urgency in my voice.

'Why?' she queried.

'Stop!' I exclaimed and ducked under the dashboard waiting for the expected collision.

Because of the pantomime going on at her side reluctantly she braked and turning to me impatiently, asked, 'Whatever's wrong with you?'

'You're so involved with steering that you are not looking at the road. We nearly had a smash then,' I answered sharply. I opened the door and got out. Taking my wallet out I extracted some money and said, 'You can go to the driving school, I'm not coming with you any more.'

I never taught her driving after that. I learnt the hard way that the husband is not the best person to tutor his wife because of the closeness of the relationship. From this I received the insight that I was probably not the best person to lead Susheila to Christ. Not by direct pressure, anyway. So I had a word with the Lord about it.

I said, 'Lord, I know with absolute certainty that you are alive but I want you to tell Susheila as well. I leave it in your hands. You're getting no help from me; you must do it on your own.'

So I never left a Bible open at the right place either on the sideboard or under her pillow for her to pick up and read, as it were, by accident. She became a Christian three years after this with no help from me. What a joy family life is when husband and wife are Christians together. They are united not only by the ties of marriage but also by the bond of Christian love.

We have two boys now and I thank God that Jesus found me before I began to raise a family, because my children love the Lord and possess the resulting joy and peace. We had a caravan holiday in North Wales one year. I remember my two boys were playing in the caravan and one pushed the other into my wife who nearly fell down. The youngest turned round and said,' Don't push mummy because if she dies we've only got daddy left!'

'Oh no,' said the other one, 'we've got Jesus left!'

What a delight it is to teach the boys in the Christian faith and as a family to enjoy the benefits of belonging to God's great family.

Not only did my conversion benefit my family life but it transformed my professional life. When I joined Lloyds as a Hindu my whole aim was to go back to India.

'When can I be the senior principal? What can I get from Lloyds?' Those were the thoughts that occupied my mind.

But when Jesus took over my life it completely changed. Now I don't want to know what I can get from my employers but what I can give them. The Christian can confidently give of his best in his work regardless of whether his boss is critical of the Christian faith or whether his workmates scorn him. Paul in Romans tells us that all things work together for good to them that love God. The Psalmist quotes God as saying, 'I will instruct you and teach you the way you should go.' God through the prophet Isaiah said, 'Fear not for I am with you; be not dismayed for I am your God.' Whatever the circumstances at work the Christian can rely on the promises of God.

A change of attitude came in my social life. You

know, when I first arrived in England I had an inferiority complex. I was very conscious not only that I was a black man but also that I was only five foot four tall. Today I walk tall because 'To all who believed him he gave power to become children of God.' I know that I am one of the adopted sons of the King of Kings before whom all earthly monarchs will have to bow the knee. What a dignity that gives to me. I used to have a vacuum in my heart in the shape of God but now I hold my head high because by royal appointment I am an ambassador for Christ, the Saviour of the world.

Jesus said one day to his disciples 'Rejoice that your names are written in Heaven.' My name, too, is written in the Lamb's book of life. I rejoice with all my heart and I do not feel inferior any longer.

9: Why Jesus?

When I was at university our physics professor once remarked that Jesus is the only way.

But what I thought he said was, 'My religion is good and your religion is no good.'

It is not what is said but what the listener hears that is important. My parents had taught me that Hinduism was one of the best and oldest religions in the world and the professor was telling me that Christianity was the best. Whom should I believe? My loving parents or a stranger? Since the professor did not explain to me what he meant by his statement I thought that he was being presumptous.

Frequently people have asked me, 'Vijay, could you not have found God by being a good Hindu and obeying your religion? For that matter, you could have accepted Jesus, read the Bible, learned from Christ's teaching and still remained a good Hindu. Hinduism does not prohibit you from doing just that, so why change?'

Without being aware of it they have answered their own question; I did read the Bible.

A cousin of mine was strongly attacking the Bible one day when I asked him, 'Have you read it?'

Quickly came the reply, 'Of course not. If I read it I would be converted!'

You have heard the expression, 'Curiosity killed

the cat!' Well, out of curiosity after my question, read it he did and he was converted.

When I had problems I told God. Then I read the Bible and from my Bible reading I found out for myself the answers to my questions. So the Bible was the main channel through which God led me to the truth.

In this chapter I would like to share with you how I, a Hindu who persecuted Christians in India, and would have been frightened at the very thought of becoming a Christian, became convinced beyond any doubt that Jesus is the Way for Hindus, Moslems, Buddhists or anyone, as well as for Christians.

I had never had any doubt in my mind that there is only one God, that the One who created the Hindus is the same as the One who made the Christians and who sustains the universe. I was glad, therefore, when I read in the Bible, 'You are worthy, our Lord and God, to receive glory and honour and power, for you created all things and by your will they were created and have their being.'

My heart leapt with joy when I read that the main purpose of God in creating me, a Hindu, was to give him praise and glory and to accomplish his purpose in me. This was made more clear when I read, 'For God so loved the world that he gave his only Son, that whoever believes in him shall not perish but have eternal life. For God did not send his Son into the world to condemn the world, but to save the world through him.'

The love God has for me is so intense that I fail to find a parallel to it. God has blessed me with two wonderful sons, although they sometimes make their mother think that she has two boys too many! I love

97

them more than anybody else in this world. One day I realised that God loves me more than I love my children: I don't expect a greater love than that. Let me explain how I came to that conclusion.

Suppose you and my son went to Wales, pot-holing, and met with an accident whilst down in the cave. The rescue team above realised that only one could be pulled to safety in time and called on me to make the choice. How much must I care for you if I decide to let my son die in your place? Then, how much greater is God's love for me, a Hindu, because he need not have died for me. Moreover, he does not even point a finger at me. 'For God did not send his Son into the world to condemn the world, but to save the world through him.'

Jesus does not say, 'Vijay, you are a naughty boy; you never went to church, nor read the Bible daily; you never obeyed my commandments.' Instead, he says, 'Vijay, I know all about you, what a terrible man you are, how selfish and self-centred you have been. There is nothing about you that I do not know. I know even your thoughts. Nevertheless, I came not to condemn you but to save you.' When I made a mess of my life, he came to pick up the pieces and start anew, to instruct me and guide me in the way I should go and to counsel me with his eyes upon me.

Naturally, the immediate thoughts that came into my mind were, 'If that is true, why am I faced with so many problems? Why are my prayers not answered? Where is God?'

Again, I found the answer in God's Word. 'Surely the arm of the Lord is not too short to save, nor his ear too dull to hear. But your iniquities have hidden his face from you, so that he will not hear.'

You see, I had disobeyed God. I had broken his commandments. Not only had I broken his laws, but I had also not lived as I wanted to live. On New Year's Day, I would make resolutions, such as:-

I shall get up early in the morning.

I shall always help my wife with the washing up.

I shall help my children with their homework.

I shall tell no lies.

I shall not be a cheat.

By February, I had broken half my promises, and by March I had broken all of them. Even though I had lowered God's laws to my level, I had not obeyed a single one of them. Suddenly, it came to my mind that 'sin' was not what I had imagined it to be. I remembered that while I was in India I had laughed at Christians who talked so much about their 'sin'. I called them 'guilty sinners'. I with my disciplined life, had never considered myself a sinner. Of course, I had failed at one time or another, but then, who had not? I looked at the word 'sin' afresh and found that it had 'I' in the centre. In the same way I was in the centre of everything I did. As far as I was concerned, the whole universe revolved around me. I had wilfully disobeyed God. Many a time, consciously or unconsciously, I had had my own way instead of being under God's rule.

Then I read, 'All have sinned and fall short of the glory of God.' The Archbishop, the Pope, the clergymen, all holy men, whatever faith they may belong to, in fact, everyone who has lived on this earth, with the exception only of Jesus, has been guilty of sin in the eyes of God, along with me. The fact that I never felt guilty did not stop me from being guilty.

If your friends knew all that comes into your mind

it is likely that you would have no friends left. If my wife knew all the thoughts that go through my mind, she would divorce me on the spot! Such is our real self in the sight of God.

'The wages of sin is death but the free gift of God is eternal life in Christ Jesus our Lord,' says his Word. I knew that I would have to die one day. Hinduism clearly asserts that every Hindu will have to face death and answer God for all that he has done in his life; not a very comfortable thought. If God had recorded all that I had done on his 'video tape', I did not want him to play it back to me. That in itself would be enough to accuse me through and through. God would be perfectly justified in sending me to hell.

Death is the most democratic thing in all the world, for everyone will have to face it one day. Not only would I have to die, but I realised that I was already dead to God spiritually. However, the free gift of God is eternal life in Christ Jesus our Lord. In other words, God has built a bridge for me to reach him today, by taking 'I' from the centre of my life and writing 'Christ' in its place.

The apostle Peter explains how this was accomplished: 'For Christ died for sins once for all, the righteous for the unrighteous, to bring you to God. He was put to death in the body but made alive by the Spirit.' He covered my sin on the cross. The first accident I had in my car was at High Wycombe on my way to speak at Oxford University. Soon after I remember my insurance agent consoling me by saying, 'Don't worry, Vijay, it is covered.' Yes, my failures are covered on the cross. The Psalmist tells me, 'Blessed is he whose transgressions are forgiven, whose sins are covered.' It is if my video tape in heaven, with all its recording of my life, has been completely wiped clean, absolutely blank. Paul says in Romans, 'Therefore there is now no condemnation for those who are in Christ Jesus.'

'For it is by grace you have been saved, through faith – and this not from yourselves, it is the gift of God – not by works, so that no one can boast.' All my life I had been trying to build bridges to God: religion, meditation, yoga, good works and many other things such as going to church, reading the Bible, saying my prayers, being baptised and confirmed, in short 'doing works'. Now I could see that the only bridge whereby any man can reach God is the one built from God's side, the Cross, and the only thing man has to give God is his sin. I found that it is here, at the Cross, that God himself took the punishment that I deserved to receive.

I have always been allergic to examinations! They made such a mark on my life that I often had nightmares about sitting for them: the agony of it all when you find that you cannot answer a single question. When you are having a nightmare, you cannot even see the question paper clearly. I would wake up with sweat pouring over my brow and, to my great relief, realise that I was safe in my bed. As a Hindu, I knew that I had to sit for the final exam with God, an interview that I was sure to fail and now, here was Jesus telling me that I had passed. Hooray! No final exam, no condemnation. I was indeed on the winning side.

Now what is this life I received from Jesus when I, a Hindu, came to him? 'Therefore if anyone is in Christ he is a new creation; the old has gone, the new has come.' I am not a patched-up convert but a new creation. Jesus has not only covered my failures, but, by the power of his Spirit, he has also re-created my spirit my making it alive.

One day I read the story of Nicodemus' night-time encounter with Jesus. Religiously, he was in a class of his own, far more than anything I could claim. What surprised me most when I read that passage was that Jesus was answering Nicodemus even before he asked any questions. God could see into Nicodemus's heart even before a word was uttered. In this story Jesus was telling me, 'Vijay, it is not enough for you to acknowledge me as God. Unless you are born again spiritually by the work of my Spirit, you are dead as a door nail, however religious you may try to become. You have a body, soul and spirit, but your spirit is dead. You have to be reborn of the Spirit to enter my kingdom, which happens now, not when you die. Vijay, I am the Resurrection and the Life; he who believes in me though he dies yet shall he live and whoever believes and lives by me shall never die. Fear not that your life shall come to an end but rather fear it may never have a beginning.' I consider that the word 'believe' as used by Jesus means 'live by him'.

The question that may come into your mind as you read this, 'What happened then?' Well, a good deal. You will know the truth if you read the words of the apostle John. 'Yet to all who received him, to those who believed in his name, he gave the right to become children of God – children born not of natural descent, nor of human decision or a husband's will, but born of God.' I was born again into God's family. Finally, I have found God. I have passed from death to life.

Why is it then that some who wished they had belonged to Jesus never crossed the bridge? It is true that God calls people in different ways. He finds them in completely different circumstances. There are no set patterns, methods, formulae or even prayer words that take us to God, but God deals with each one of us in a unique way. It is not the words that we utter as prayer, but the heart behind the prayer which he looks at.

I wanted to belong to God so much that in my heart I was willing to pay any price. This is what it actually cost me. Imagine I came to your house with a kidney machine to sell when you are on the point of dying through kidney failure and you enquire how much it costs. If my reply is that I will exchange it for the rubbish in your back garden would you consider it too great a price to pay? Wouldn't you be only too willing to pay any price for that machine? The cost I had to pay Jesus was the rubbish in my back garden; my sin, my selfish nature, all that made me unhappy and made my life a misery. I could have cherished my rubbish and said 'no' to him as some people do, but that thought never even crossed my mind.

There was another reason for my not worrying about the cost at that time. An event that happened in the Indian Ocean illustrates it. A tanker and a methane gas carrier collided along the coast of South Africa and they became potential bombs. A small spark would have been sufficient to blow the two ships to pieces. Immediately, all the crew dived into the water in order to get as far away from the ships as possible, all the crew, that is, except for two seamen. These men did not think the situation was that critical. Within twenty minutes, however, the expected explosion did occur and killed both of them.

What the people who jumped into the sea had not realised, though, was that the place of the accident had a reputation for being shark infested; for them it was a case of jumping from the frying pan into the fire. Their anguish did not last long, however, because the rescue team were soon on the scene. When the ladders were dropped from the hovering helicopters, those in the water did not hesitate and call out, 'Are you sure it is safe for us to come on board? Are you insured with Lloyds's? Can you take us to safety?' No, instead they jumped on board with never a second's thought, only too anxious to be rescued. To me, the death of Christ on the Cross came like that rescue operation and I was willing to put my whole weight on it.

That rescue operation is not limited to a privileged few but is for everyone who is willing to take up Christ's offer. If you are not rescued it is not because Jesus has rejected you, but because you have rejected him. The voyage may be rough at times, but he is at the helm to take us safely to God for ever.

10: Comparisons and contrasts

When in earlier chapters I described the various facets of Hinduism you must, I feel sure, have been struck by the fact that there are a few similarities to Christianity. This is often pounced on by agnostics who say, 'There you are, look, the religions of the world have comparable beliefs, they are as good as each other, they all lead to truth.' The atheists say, 'The religions of the world contain the same fictitious legends and therefore that proves that they are all as bad as one another and that there is no God.'

The truth, I am persuaded, is far otherwise. Not that I believe there should be any intolerance on the part of Christians of others' sincerely held faith. There is no room for scorn. Remember that Paul and Barnabas at Lystra boldly proclaimed, 'The living God has not left himself without witness'. Every human being is made in the Divine image and there is that of God in everyone capable of responding to spiritual reality. Hinduism contains some partial truths and much spirituality. Christians could well emulate the zeal shown by devout Hindus in their daily devotions.

Nevertheless there is a uniqueness about Christianity. Jesus said 'No man comes unto the Father but by me.' A bold claim indeed but it lies at the heart of Christianity. The Christian faith can admit no rivals. Jesus Christ, and he alone, is Lord. Therefore there can be no question of the synthesis with other religions that some people talk about. The Christian faith is missionary in its nature though Christians must approach those of other faiths with sympathy born of understanding and above all with deep love. That missionaries have not always done so is a blot upon the Christian Church and a denial of him whose very name is love.

I want us now to look at some of the similarities and differences. First, then, the affinities. A tenet of the caste system is that the higher the caste, the greater the responsibility. More is rightly expected of a Brahmin than of a peasant labourer. That has its counterpart in Christianity where the greater one's understanding and experience of the faith, the greater one's moral and spiritual obligations. Jesus made this crystal clear in his parable of the unjust steward when he said, 'Unto whomsoever much is given, of him shall much be required.' A child brought up in a Christian home and the atmosphere of a spiritually alive church will find that the claims of God press more heavily upon him than on someone who has always lived in the pagan environment of a city slum, surrounded by evil and never hearing the name of the Deity except in blasphemous oaths. And justifiably so, for 'Shall not the Judge of all the earth do right?'

Yoga is a peculiarly Indian art. It is essentially a strict religious discipline. The physical exercises connected with it are for the purpose of inducing peace in the mind and developing the life of the spirit. The idea is that the body's subservience to the spirit is established in order that it may make a positive contribution to the spiritual well-being of the participant. It is quite easy to see the correspondence between this and various statements in the New Testament about self-control. A little later we will look at the difference.

On the surface there is an even greater similarity between the fakir on his bed of nails and Paul's words to the church at Corinth about bringing his body into subjection and to the Roman church regarding the wisdom of mortifying the deeds of the body. This resemblance, however, is a superficial one. In other instances Paul makes it quite plain that he would not dream of disparaging the body and its functions for this is God's creation. In writing to the Colossians, for example, he uses strong, almost scornful words against ascetic practices which neglect the body.

Maya is the Hindu concept that the material world is an illusion. It might be said that this is a point of difference rather than a parallel thought since Christianity has been described as the most materialistic religion in the world. I agree that there is a certain dissimilarity which is quite important. We will look at this shortly but here for the moment we are concerned with affinities. Materialism as understood by Christian doctrine is the idea that matter is all-important; that nothing exists apart from matter; that we should concentrate on non-religious, secular interests instead of on spiritual ones. This dogma both Hinduism and Christianity emphatically reject. It is not without relevance that recent scientific work has revealed that the material universe does not possess the solid reality previously ascribed to it.

We have noticed earlier that the goal of the individual Hindu is the merging of his soul with Brahma who is the Ultimate Reality behind everything. Christianity, on the other hand, never thinks of the human personality coalescing with the Divine nature; that, to the Christian, would appear almost blasphemous. 'We know that we shall be like him' says John but that is very different from being identical. Nevertheless, there is a certain likeness between this teaching and some very wonderful mystic passages in the New Testament. In John's gospel Jesus tells the parable of the vine and states that if Christians are to bear fruit they have to abide in him. In his first letter John declares 'He that has the Son has life'. Paul in his letter to the Galations boldly states that it is not he who lives but Christ in him. In his development of the doctrine of the atonement Paul sets out the concept of faith-union with the crucified Christ, so that Christians share the experience of suffering, dying and rising again.

The Hindu doctrine of *Karma* is similar to the viewpoint of Job's friends. You will remember that they were convinced that Job's suffering must have been the result of some undeclared sin in his life. They were applying the moral law of cause and effect, which is what *Karma* is, in a rigid, mechanistic way that was incompatible with truth. Nevertheless, the basic tenet that there is a moral law woven into the very fabric of the universe which man offends at his peril, is entirely congruous with Christian teaching.

Both religions have sacrifices. In some Indian temples animal sacrifices are offered to the gods. In Christianity the sacrifices are two-fold. On the human side there is the offering of a broken spirit and a contrite heart; on the Divine side there is nothing less than the utter self-giving of God himself in Christ. Hindu sacrifices resemble more the Judaic offerings of the Old Testament.

These comparisons only serve to highlight the many and varied points of difference between the two religions. A few have already surfaced even as we looked at the similarities. There are many more. Hinduism for example, has thirty-three thousand gods, whereas Christians worship one God only expressed as a Trinity, God the Father, God the Son and God the Holy Spirit

Hinduism has no founder. From this fact stem some of the vital contrasts between it and Christianity. The latter originated as an historic revelation by God who himself came to earth in the person of Jesus. Christians believe that they cannot know God unless he firsts takes the initative and reveals himself. So the baby at Bethlehem is a fact of history. Hindus try to attain communion with him whom they regard as impersonal reality by self-realisation. It is a very far cry from the Father of our Lord Jesus Christ.

As a natural result there are no clear-cut credal statements and as we have noted earlier Hindus can make their own interpretations of what is right and what is wrong. This, of course, leads to a miscellany of beliefs. It may astonish you to learn that Hindus happily accept wrong-doing from their own gods for, since God is in all things, there is no clear separation of good and evil. Yet in their epic *Ramayana* a battle is portrayed between good and evil. The more you learn about Hinduism the more you will realise it contains many contradictions. It is inconceivable to Christians that the Creator could be the same as creation or God be good and evil but that is how Brahman is understood.

It follows from this that there is no universal moral code. Each person's religious duties are different. What wonderful scope that provides an evil man: 'I had no option but to do this, it was my dharma'. There is another implication. If there is no distinction between Creator and created this means that the religious life consists of finding God within oneself. This could even mean worshipping the reflection seen in the mirror! Of course, we all know that there are many non Hindus who in their vanity do adore their own image but however seriously they may take themselves I do not imagine that they actually make a religion out of it.

The caste system is clearly incompatible with Christianity. It is good to know that there has been increasingly strong pressure within Hinduism itself in recent years to change the system which has become more and more an anachronism in the modern world and has always been morally wrong. In fact, it is now an offence to discriminate on grounds of caste but passing a law does not of itself necessarily change human behaviour and the tradition of thousands of years. What probably surprises a Westerner is the fact that a faith which in general is very tolerant has so much rigidity in its thinking about something so socially divisive as caste.

Not that Christians can afford to be complacent, for the Christian Church has had its share of class distinctions throughout history from slavery to pew rents and private galleries in churches. But these alienating factors, unlike those of Hinduism, were sinful errors and not a true expression of the faith of the people involved. In Galatians we find a soul-stirring exposition by Paul of the supreme irrelevance of class consciousness ending with the memorable words, 'You are all one in Christ Jesus.' It is interesting to note in passing that in India the Brahmin priest stands at the highest point of the social scale which is certainly not true of Christian priests and ministers in the secular climate of England today. Not that that need worry followers of the One who exhorted his disciples to be servants one of another. High caste religious leaders frequently fall into the sin of pride and this is almost inevitable in view of the nature of the caste system.

Spreading the good news of the Gospel is a vital element of Christianity not least because it was the express command of Jesus. The Christian Church exists for mission. Individual Christians have a great compassion for people throughout the world living in the darkness of ignorance and sin. They long that everyone may receive the salvation freely available for all. But the exclusive nature of Hinduism precludes its followers from having any missionary fervour. Like Moslems they tend to be fatalistic – 'What will be, will be.'

Their idea of salvation is vastly different from Christian doctrine. Salvation for the Hindu comes from contemplation and right thinking and is achieved when the pinnacle of the mystic state is reached and the human soul is united with Brahman. They believe that they can go a long way towards earning salvation by a strict performance of their religious duties. There is very little consciousness of personal sin against a holy God; at most there is merely a guilty conscience if a religious obligation has been neglected. The sweet and wonderful world of forgiveness forms no part of Hinduism. What a difference from Christian belief. Christianity teaches that it is totally impossible to earn salvation. Christianity teaches, too, the exceeding sinfulness of sin. There is nothing, but absolutely nothing, that unaided man can do about sin. He has first of all to realise the hopelessness of his position. When he has reached a state of self-despair, God can do something for him. God in Christ has entered the world in order to save the world and on the Cross Jesus has identified himself with the human predicament in order that he might bring us to God. What a contrast from Krishna who, although he is called the preserver, said he had come to destroy sinners. Our Saviour, on the other hand, said, 'I came not to call the righteous but sinners to repentance.' The yawning chasm between the two religions is at once evident.

Hindus speak of faith in God but the origin, content and direction of this is poles apart from Christian faith. This is because a Hindu starts from within himself.

I remember a fellow hospital patient who, seeing the Bible in my hand, remarked 'I've got faith, too.'

'That is good, that makes two of us. Let's talk about it,' I replied.

I soon found out that he believed that somehow or other he was going to come out of his operation scot free. The faith found in Hinduism, like that of my fellow patient, originates from within and depends on the devotee's ability to believe. This is quite contrary to Christian faith which is not a blind optimism but stems from God's power to fulfil what he has promised. The faith of a Christian rests neither on his own prayers nor on his own personal commitment but on the finished work of Christ on the Cross. The direction of his faith is towards God's mercy and not to *Dharma* or good works.

Yoga has become very popular in the West in recent years. It cannot be too emphatically stated, however, that yoga is a practice inseparably connected with the Hindu religion. Often the words which are used to induce a trance-like state, the mantras, are the names of Hindu gods. Moreover, there are very real dangers. Hallucinations can be experienced similar to those which follow the taking of drugs. Yoga, in my considered opinion, is definitely not for the Christian. Christian meditation is quite different in that it does not neglect the use of reason whereas yoga abandons the process of thought.

A characteristic Indian hypothesis is that time moves in circles. Western thought generally thinks of time as proceeding in a straight line. Perhaps you think that this is essentially a philosophic matter rather than a religious one. Well, maybe, but it certainly has religious undertones. Hindu belief that souls return repeatedly to this earth to occupy a succession of bodies is a practical application of the 'circles' theory, of returning again and again, like a gramophone record, to a place near the starting point. 'Going in circles' is a phrase which to Western minds means aimlessness and getting nowhere. The thought of time progessing in a straight line, on the other hand, is suggestive of purpose. Certainly the Bible discloses God's progressive revelation to mankind. And Christian doctrine thinks of time as moving steadily forward to the final consummation of all things when time itself will come to an end.

Hindus believe that marriage continues in the spiritual world. It is an attractive idea, especially to those who have lost their life partner. No doubt many Christians would like to think it were true. Jesus, however, makes it clear that there is no giving in marriage in Heaven, simply because relationships there are on another plane altogether. Although the New Testament gives surprisingly little information about relationships in heaven with loved ones, we may take it as entirely reasonable that we shall meet and know each other again and join together in the ecstatic joys of Heaven. Love is supreme and for it to operate it must have tangible objects on which to lavish affection. It may be objected that God alone will be the goal of our love but such a viewpoint belittles his creative activity in making men and women in his own image with the capacity to love. To cease to have loving fellowship simply because we are in the spiritual world would be unthinkable.

Hinduism, in common with other Oriental religions, thinks of matter as being evil. We are clothed with a physical body which we must suffer with patience. The Biblical standpoint, however, is that matter is a Divine creation. God looked at the world he had created and he saw that it was good. There can be no question of it being evil. What the Bible does recognise is that there is imperfection in the world due to sin, but that is a very different matter.

As I have looked once again at the faith of my fathers, with, I believe, a sympathetic but fair appraisal, I can see that the contrasts with Christianity are much more numerous and serious than the comparisons. I can see and I hope that you can, too, that the Christian faith is not only unquestionably unique but that it reveals the only true way to God, through Jesus Christ the Saviour of the world.

11: Saved to serve

When I began looking for property in the Essex town in which I now live I asked the estate agent if there were other Indian families in the locality. I was greatly relieved to learn that there were none. This may seem a surprising attitude to take, even one to be deprecated, but England was now my home and I longed to be absorbed into its culture. The last thing I wanted was to become part of a foreign ghetto which would act as a barrier between my family and English customs.

Not that I was unconcerned about those of my own race. When I was first converted I had an overwhelming desire to return to India and tell my fellow countrymen what Christianity was all about. I felt that so many of them were not so much rejecting my new-found faith as misunderstanding it. I was wildly enthusiastic to go back and restore the lines of communications between Christian and Hindu. But God quickly showed me he had another task lined up for me. Taking the Gospel to Indians in England? No, not even that. It was to preach to English people themselves and tell them the way of salvation. But first I had to overcome an obstacle; this was my ingrained conviction that all the English were already Christians. The Lord soon enlightened me on this point!

My Christian work began very quietly and unobtrusively in unspectacular ways. Neighbouring churches wanted to hear the story of my conversion and that was too good an evangelistic opportunity to miss for by now I had come to realise that there might well be unconverted folk in the congregation. I knew that even being a regular churchgoer was no guarantee that a man or woman possessed a personal faith in Jesus as Saviour and Lord.

Some of the invitations came from schools and colleges and here I really began to come into my own. It seemed that I had a special ministry to young people and I was not at all conscious of the much talked about 'generation gap'. As I mused over this strange phenomenon the penny suddenly dropped. Twenty-five years earlier the Lord must have been preparing me for this time by giving me practice in expressing concepts in simple terms and concrete imagery as I helped my wife's elder sister with her homework. I felt that this was surely the Lord's doing and it was marvellous in my eyes.

My style of speaking appeared to go down well with the adults also which I suppose is not all that surprising for after all, what are adults but grown-up children? Coming to Christianity from Hinduism and having no English reserve I brought a freshness, vividness and bounding enthusiasm to the exposition of the Gospel. Gradually I found myself going further and further afield as the news spread that there was a Hindu in the Church of England! This did not present me with insuperable problems for I still loved travel but it did mean that I had to devote more and more of my time to preparing talks and giving them, not to mention time spent in travelling. People began to say that I only went to work in the City in order to get money for my collections and there was more than an element of truth in this. What a change from the man of earlier years who lived for his daily work. Today, my ambition has been completely reorientated and I can truly echo Paul's words, 'For me to live is Christ'. In the Indian language 'Vijay' means absolute victory. To help people who have difficulty in remembering my first name I have devised a simple agnostic, 'Victory in Jesus always yours' and this I have proved to be true. Yes, I believe that Christians have been given the ammunition to win the battle against evil. The Word of God, for example, is so powerful that it is dynamite.

We had a bomb scare at Lloyds one day. Early on a Monday morning someone rang up to say that the building would be blown up at ten o'clock. The premises were systematically searched but nothing untoward was found. It was then thought possible that someone might attempt to bring a bomb in, so two policemen and our sergeant-porter inspected everyone who entered. When I arrived there was a long queue waiting to get in. Eventually my turn came.

My friend the sergeant asked me, 'Vijay, what have you got in that attache case?'

'Dynamite,' I replied.

The two policemen jumped forward, snatched the case, opened it and out fell – a black-covered Bible!

'There you are, that is dynamite,' I beamed. 'Read it and you'll never be the same again.'

As I have travelled around I have found that people gravely misunderstand the relationship between science and Christianity. Many non-

Christians think that modern science is opposed to Christianity but of course this is not so at all. Science, for example, can never prove or disprove the existence of God because this is an area outside its province and this is well understood by scientists themselves.

There are many eminent scientists today who are committed Christians. As an engineer I have to read technical magazines in my office. I recall once reading in a scientific journal a whole article devoted to scientists who believe in God. I myself would say that there are more Christians in the scientific world than in any other profession.

I was talking one day to a scientist friend of mine and he emphatically stated that faith was essential to scientists. He explained how he himself was analysing sodium light by measuring the wavelength of a ray. By ascertaining a similar wavelength in the light emanating from a star it is possible to deduce that it has sodium. We have not been to the star but we know by faith that the star contains sodium.

That reminds me of a story from my Indian days. A clever Hindu student was invited by one of the professors to tea. As he walked into the sitting room there was a model of the solar system, exactly to scale. He was most intrigued.

'Who made it?' he enquired.

The professor replied, 'It just happened'.

'But someone must have made it,' he insisted.

The professor remained silent and suddenly the clever chap realised what the professor was saying. The tutor handed a Bible to this student and asked him to read Psalm 14:1.

He read aloud, 'The fool hath said in his heart,

"There is no God."'' This effectually silenced him.

As a Hindu when I try to prove God I find I have to comprehend him within the limitations of my imagination. Yet the universe is vast. Four billion light years away are the stars created by God and discovered by scientists through radio telescopes. How can we prove God with our five senses? We are not meant to do it. God's existence cannot be proved but must be revealed because God is infinite and we are finite. A finite being cannot measure the Infinite.

I was once speaking to seventy boys of the Upper Sixth Form of a comprehensive school at Bath. I explained that I am a senior engineer surveyor working in the City of London and that my job is to approve the design of crankshafts, boilers and engines so that I have mathematics at my fingertips. To prove it I asked them to give me a number.

Somebody shouted out '425'.

Immediately I wrote the square of 425 on the black-board behind.

Then I demanded a bigger number.

Somebody called '827' and quick as a flash I wrote the square of that number on the board.

Next, I enquired, 'What other calculation would you like me to do?'

A boy asked, 'What is the square root of their summation?'

I turned round and in a second wrote the answer down. By then I could see the headmaster, chaplain and boys sitting with their mouths wide open in total disbelief. What they did not realise was that I had an electronic calculator on the rostrum in front of me. They could not see it from down below. As I lifted up the calculator and told them that there is no magic in it I could hear one long groan from the crowd in front of me.

I was not telling any lies because all I said was that I had mathematics at my fingertips! All I had to do was to push the buttons and the answer was lit up in red numbers on the small screen in a matter of seconds. I explained to them I did not know how the calculator worked but there was no magic in it.

I then said that I had no idea how God raised Jesus from the dead but the resurrection is a fact of history and there is no magic in it.

A boy from the front row shouted out, 'What does that mean, Sir? Don't blind us with science. How does that prove that Jesus is alive?'

Well, he was right up to a point, but he had jumped to a conclusion without hearing the complete answer. I asked the group whether there were any there who had seen an atom being split. If I had stressed that there is no nuclear fission they would have questioned my credentials. But they had never seen an atom being split; nor have I, for that matter, even though I am a member of the British Nuclear Energy Society. There are many nuclear scientists and physicists whom I know who have never seen an atom being split but we believe because when we start the reactor it produces steam to generate electrical power and that is the proof. The evidence is so real that it would be foolish to deny that it happens.

In a similar way Jesus said, 'But you will receive power when the Holy Spirit comes on you; and you will be my witnesses.' The evidence of the power of the Holy Spirit of God in my life is so real that my faith is by no means a blind, unreasoning process. I do not have to know the theories of solar energy to enjoy the sunshine. My faith is not even based on how I feel but on the facts of the crucifixion and resurrection of Jesus. Yes, Jesus Christ is indeed alive today and I do not have to wait till I die to prove it in my life.

I usually find that young people are attentive and responsive. Sometimes, however, one or two belligerent questioners can make it hard going but I persevere in sowing the seed and do not expect always to see an immediate harvest. That is an issue in God's hands.

I am less tolerant of apathy in professing Christians. I went one day to a college at one of our universities where a group of about twenty Christian undergraduates had asked me to speak to them on Christian living. To my dismay they came and sat in front of me with no notebooks and no Bibles. I saw red.

I stood up and asked, 'What are you here for? To be entertained? To receive a passing inspiration? It took me twenty hours to prepare this talk; you might at least do me the courtesy of taking notes. If my boss gives me instructions and I say, "I have enjoyed your little talk" he would kick me out for being impudent. Can you play tennis without a racquet? I do not propose to begin until you have obtained pens, notebooks and Bibles.' They got them!

Another point about preaching is that even mature churchgoers do not always seem to appreciate the fact that an address should be related to the needs of listeners.

One Sunday evening I went to a Free Church where I had been asked to give an evangelistic address. I could sense that I was before a congregation of Christians.

I began by asking them, 'How many of you are here for the first time? Put your hands up if you are.'

There were none.

'How many,' I asked, 'attend here regularly?'

All hands shot up.

'Then you do not need an evangelistic address,' I said. 'I'm going to tear up my talk and speak on spiritual growth instead.'

In my evangelistic talks I usually make an appeal for full commitment and ask those who wish to respond to write their name and address on slips of paper which have been distributed to all present. Within a few days I write a letter to each one enclosing booklets which explain the way of salvation and provide a simple course of Bible study. I also give them details of further follow-up booklets which they can procure for themselves if they so desire. The purchase of Christian literature to give away is a heavy item of annual expenditure but when I receive donations I put these into a special fund for book purchase and the Lord sees that I and my family are never in need.

One of my most challenging recent engagements was to visit a home to speak to about twenty-four young couples where in each case one partner was a non-Christian. I hope and pray that fruit will come from that encounter. I could at least speak from personal experience.

Soon after I became a Christian, long before I had any idea that I would be called to speak, I had a strong desire to study in depth, so I joined the only course available that time at London Bible College. It happened to be homiletics, that is, instruction in the art of preaching and I gained distinction in the certificate which was awarded.

Some time afterwards the Principal, the Rev. Gilbert Kirby, was kind enough to invite me to return and preach at the Sunday morning service in the College. I was petrified that I might not measure up to the standard of his teaching, but placed myself in God's hands. I began with trepidation but soon even forgot that the Principal was by my side. When I finished I realised that I had just about broken every rule in the book! Such was the response from the students, however, that two years later a Japanese girl came up to me at Cambridge University and told me everything that I had said that morning. When God communicates he can use us in spite of ourselves and we need not always stick to the man-made rules.

A person becoming a Christian is like a big chain with many links. As I speak about Jesus to others I know that I have to provide only that link which God wants me to make and he will do the rest with the help of others. 'Some may plant, some may water and some may harvest, but it is God who gives life and growth.' It is from this steady trickle of people who respond to the claims of Christ that I get the most joy.

Engagements on this scale represent a large slice of leisure time. Even I am sometimes staggered by the number of addresses I somehow manage to give but the Lord enables me to squeeze the maximum out of every minute. There are friends who are concerned for my health but I laugh at their fears. I would much rather wear out than rust out. After many threats, my vicar, the Rev. Miles Thomson, one day stalked into my house and asked me for my correspondence file, announcing that from then on he was going to decide just how many appointments I should take because he wanted me to live a bit longer! I accepted his role as my spiritual leader and am grateful for his voluntary help, in spite of his own busy life, to keep the avalanche of requests under control.

You may think that I do this work because I enjoy public speaking but this is not the case at all. Despite my long experience I still have butterflies every time I stand up to speak and if the Lord were to make clear to me that he no longer required this work no one would be more pleased than I. Yet satisfying and meaningful rewards come from time to time as people write to tell me of deeper commitments to Christ.

I think for example of a fine young doctor in Southern England who runs a fellowship group in his home but who with characteristic Anglican diffidence did not feel able to talk freely and intimately to the members about their own spiritual condition. How thrilled he was when they showed their willingness to read the Bible openly together and when some bore public witness to their faith for the first time while others yielded their lives to Christ.

Sometimes I hear of people I met years before and make contact with them again. At a recent Synod I was in conversation with another member and was saddened to learn that his brother, who lived in a Hampshire village and whom I had met four years before, was dying of cancer. My informant wanted to offer spiritual consolation to his brother but felt somewhat inhibited in this difficult situation. On what I believe was a Divinely-guided impulse I offered to write a letter. It was a deeply-moving reply which I received back from a man who was staring Eternity in the face. He expressed the assurance that the words of my letter had come from God to minister to him and his wife in their dire need. A few days later, he died. How glad I was that I did not, as I must confess I sometimes do, delay acting on the Holy Spirit's prompting. To know that by the grace of God one has been used of him to mediate help makes all the labour infinitely worthwhile.

Of course, I have areas of failure. Like, I suspect, many other Christians I find witnessing to relatives and colleagues extremely difficult. I have, for example, two brothers in the United States. One of them came near to becoming a Christian when he lived with me in South Shields but, to my shame, used me, I was told, as a reason for not doing so because I was then still a keen devotee of Hinduism.

Once my wife's uncle and aunt visited us on their world tour. He is K. P. S. Menon who has had a distinguished career in the Indian Diplomatic Service, a career which included serving as ambassador to Russia and as India's first Foreign Secretary after Independence. He has written a number of books and has exercised considerable political influence in India's relationship with Russia. At that time we were Hindus and I can still remember his sadness as he talked about his friend's conversion to Christianity. What a triumph it would have been for him if he had understood what being a real Christian means. Regrettably, I was not in a position to explain this to him then.

Someone asked me recently how I got on in my witness at work. Ruefully I admitted to what I felt was near total failure in this aspect of my Christian life. I think that when my initial enthusiasm bubbled over in the office some of my colleagues probably considered me as a 'nut' case, a kind of religious maniac. I remember one Christmas in those early days when the office was gaily decorated and there was a general air of festivity. I thought I would point out what Christmas really meant and boldly pinned up a poster depicting the Nativity scene and asking 'Have you any room for Jesus?' It was not very well received. A protesting deputation went to the head of the section and asked for it to be removed. I was summoned into his presence and told that my poster would have to be taken down because it was giving offence. The sad fact was that the protests came, as I understood it, not from the agnostics and humanists, but from some of the churchgoers.

There was, however, one area of my Christian work which did receive some recognition in the office. One day in 1970 Richard Bewes, who was then vicar of the church to which I belonged at Harold Wood, asked me to put my name forward for the General Synod, the governing body of the Church of England. I agreed on the understanding that, apart from producing a sheet identifying myself and my ecclesiastical viewpoint, I would do no canvassing for I believed that if it was God's will for me I would get in anyway. After I was elected the managing director called me into his office to offer his congratulations and to say that he was proud such an honour had come to a member of his staff. A tangible result was that I was granted two weeks' leave of absence to enable me to attend Synod while I was to take the third week from my holiday.

I found the Synod debates interesting although views were sometimes expressed which dismayed me. I soon learnt that if I wanted to make an impact and steer a motion to a successful conclusion a simple, direct approach seldom worked. So I began to use guile, becoming 'wise as a serpent' but, I hope, 'harmless as a dove'.

One subject which was of aspecial interest to me was that of religious education in State schools. There was a suggestion that in view of the large number of immigrant children of other world religions it was not right to retain compulsory scripture teaching. I told the assembly that if religious education were taken away from schools thousands of these children would be deprived of the privilege of learning the basic culture of their society because it was unlikely that much of what was said at home would be in English. I asserted that reading the Bible at school was what made Britain the best place in the world. This is a matter which I feel very strongly about.

Synod meets but three times a year and therefore most of my church work is at a less exalted, though no less important, level. I am a member of two Parochial Church Councils, a circumstance which cannot be very common. It arise through my daytime connections with St Helens in the City and my worshipping at weekends at a surburban church. Since my first real encounter with Christianity was through a lunch-hour address at St Helens it was a great joy and honour to be invited to contribute to the series myself.

This chapter has been included in this book not to show what I have done, which may come to nothing, but to share with you what Christ can do in us and through us in spite of our weaknesses, failures and shortcomings.

So the days fly by and I often wish it were possible to cram more work into every passing minute but the Lord I serve created the hours and one day will take me beyond time into his Eternity. With that thought I am content.